I0420277

S. HRG. 114–60

S. 710, THE REAUTHORIZATION OF THE NATIVE AMERICAN HOUSING ASSISTANCE AND SELF-DETERMINATION ACT OF 2015 (NAHASDA)

HEARING

BEFORE THE

COMMITTEE ON INDIAN AFFAIRS
UNITED STATES SENATE

ONE HUNDRED FOURTEENTH CONGRESS

FIRST SESSION

MARCH 18, 2015

Printed for the use of the Committee on Indian Affairs

U.S. GOVERNMENT PUBLISHING OFFICE

95–957 PDF   WASHINGTON : 2015

For sale by the Superintendent of Documents, U.S. Government Publishing Office
Internet: bookstore.gpo.gov   Phone: toll free (866) 512–1800; DC area (202) 512–1800
Fax: (202) 512–2104   Mail: Stop IDCC, Washington, DC 20402–0001

CONTENTS

S. 710, THE REAUTHORIZATION OF THE NATIVE AMERICAN HOUSING ASSISTANCE AND SELF-DETERMINATION ACT OF 2015 (NAHASDA)

WEDNESDAY, MARCH 18, 2015

U.S. SENATE,
COMMITTEE ON INDIAN AFFAIRS,
Washington, DC.

The Committee met, pursuant to notice, at 2:50 p.m. in room 628, Dirksen Senate Office Building, Hon. John Barrasso, Chairman of the Committee, presiding.

OPENING STATEMENT OF HON. JOHN BARRASSO, U.S. SENATOR FROM WYOMING

The CHAIRMAN. Good afternoon. I call this hearing to order.

Today, the Committee will examine S. 710, the Native American Housing Assistance and Self-Determination Reauthorization Act of 2015 or NAHASDA.

I introduced S. 710 on March 11. The bill is similar to past bills introduced since NAHASDA's reauthorization ended in 2013. Reauthorization of NAHASDA has been an important priority for Indian Country.

However, Indian Country has waited too long for reauthorization. For that reason, I am looking forward to the collaboration of both the House and the Senate that will make reauthorization a reality.

I especially want to thank Senator Tester for his leadership on the important issue of Indian housing. Because of his leadership and the efforts of our colleagues, we are closer to making reauthorization a reality.

The United States is responsible for improving Indian people's housing conditions. Improved housing conditions empower tribes to take greater responsibility for their own economic condition.

In 1996, NAHASDA consolidated Federal Indian housing programs into one law. NAHASDA also furthered principles of self-governance through tribal administration of Federal Indian housing programs. Although NAHASDA has empowered tribes to tackle their own housing needs, there is still a need for housing in Indian Country.

I want to welcome our panel of tribal officials and advocates. They represent an in-depth understanding of Indian Country's housing needs and how NAHASDA can address these needs.

(1)

Chairman Karen Diver is here from the Fond du Lac Band of Lake Superior Chippewa Indians. Mr. Gary Cooper is here, a Board member and Chairman of the Legislative Committee of the NAIHC. Mr. Russell Sossamon is the Executive Director of the Housing Authority of the Choctaw Nation of Oklahoma.

I want to thank all of you for joining us.

Senator Tester, would you like to make an opening statement?

STATEMENT OF HON. JON TESTER, U.S. SENATOR FROM MONTANA

Senator TESTER. I would, Mr. Chairman.

I want to thank you again for holding this hearing also and for putting together a bill that reintroduced NAHASDA.

I want to thank the witnesses for joining us today, particularly Chairwoman Karen Diver, who welcomed me to her tribal home-lands last October when I was touring Indian Country around the Country, around the United States, touring the Fond du Lac Res-ervation. I was able to see firsthand the housing conditions facing Chairwoman Diver's community, as well as some of the innovations that are taking place on the housing front. I look forward to hear-ing before this Committee what you are doing.

Housing is vital to Indian communities across the United States. When we discuss the state of Indian housing, we must describe it in the term of crisis. A great many things impact the daily lives of Native Americans, but none so more, none more so, than hous-ing.

As all members of this Committee know, the statistics concerning housing conditions in Indian Country are staggering. Homes that do exist are in disrepair and we are nowhere close to meeting the immense need for housing throughout Indian Country.

I am sure all of our tribal housing authorities could speak at length of the weight that persists and the demand in their commu-nities is not getting any smaller.

We are also seeing the trend that tribes and tribal housing au-thorities are not constructing new homes but repairing older, worn out housing stock. As the housing stock grows older, it is more cost-ly to maintain and rehab these homes, so we must grow this pro-gram that has seen level funding since its inception in 1996, nearly 20 years.

Finally, I think we need to work with all of our Federal partners and the Administration to make sure that we are improving the tools and resources to improve the housing conditions in our Indian communities.

These agencies can work together to remove duplicative and cumbersome Federal requirements that exists throughout the Fed-eral system. They can do more to help tribes and tribal housing au-thorities access existing programs and conduct more outreach and consultation to Indian Country.

Again, I want to thank you, Mr. Chairman, for putting together this proposal. I know the tribes in my home State are carefully re-viewing it. We have heard some initial concerns about any changes to Section 703 of NAHASDA in relation to training and technical assistance. We will continue to look closely at that to make it work.

In addition, this bill removes the maximum rent requirements for housing authorities. I strongly believe in self-determination. I understand the income verification process is timely and costly. The removal of the 30 percent rule, however, will raise some concerns as it decreases tenant protections in regards to rental costs.

I look forward to working with you, Mr. Chairman, and your staff to address these concerns as we move this bill through the legislative process.

Finally, I would say I think we have an opportunity here when it comes to housing to build some great partnerships with the Federal Government and local tribes. If we can do that and empower them to meet the housing needs in their individual communities, I think we will have succeeded.

Thank you, Mr. Chairman.

The CHAIRMAN. Thank you very much.

Senator Lankford?

STATEMENT OF HON. JAMES LANKFORD, U.S. SENATOR FROM OKLAHOMA

Senator LANKFORD. Thank you, Mr. Chairman.

I just want to make a brief introduction of Mr. Russell Sossamon who is from the Choctaw Nation of Oklahoma. It is the third largest tribe in the Country with over 200,000 members who are scattered all over the place. There is a unique perspective, obviously, for non-reservation tribes as the housing issues are common both in reservation and non-reservation tribes.

I appreciate him coming. It is not the first time he has testified before this Committee but we are glad to have his insight as he returns today.

Thank you, Mr. Chairman.

The CHAIRMAN. Thank you, Senator Lankford.

Senator Franken.

STATEMENT OF HON. AL FRANKEN, U.S. SENATOR FROM MINNESOTA

Senator FRANKEN. Thank you, Mr. Chairman.

It is my honor to introduce my friend, Karen Diver, Chairwoman of the Fond du Lac Band of the Lake Superior Ojibwe. Chairwoman Diver is an ideal witness to discuss the reauthorization of NAHASDA.

Under her leadership, Fond du Lac has been leading the way in addressing the housing needs of its community. Two years ago, Fond du Lac opened the first supportive housing project in the country dedicated to serving homeless veterans on Indian reservations. She has also testified before the Indian Affairs Committee before on the harsh impact of sequestration on Indian Country.

It is my pleasure to welcome Chairwoman Diver back to the Committee. I look forward to hearing from her and all the witnesses today.

Thank you.

The CHAIRMAN. Thank you, Senator Franken.

Senator Lankford.

Senator LANKFORD. Let me finish out this conversation and welcome the Cherokee Nation. We are glad to be able to have both

Choctaw and Cherokee here. We have significant relationships across the entire State.

As most folks know, in Oklahoma we have 39 recognized tribes, 38 federally-recognized and what happens with housing is obviously incredible different not only on reservation and non-reservation, but area to area within the State.

The southeast part of our State and the northeast part of our State are only unique in that they are both in Oklahoma, based on the real differences that are there. We are glad to have you here, Mr. Cooper, as well.

Thank you, Mr. Chairman.

The CHAIRMAN. Senator Heitkamp.

STATEMENT OF HON. HEIDI HEITKAMP, U.S. SENATOR FROM NORTH DAKOTA

Senator HEITKAMP. Mr. Chairman, I have just a brief comment that is kind of to lay down a marker.

I am extraordinarily interested in moving NAHASDA forward. I think it is critically important but even if we authorize NAHASDA and even if all that money gets deployed in a very short period of time, we will still have a crisis in housing in Indian Country.

Where NAHASDA is critically important for all the reasons the Chairman stated, we have to have a different and more expansive strategy to deal with the housing needs in Indian Country.

I want to thank the Chairman for bringing this forward, but also encourage further discussion about private-public partnerships, working with States to build more and more affordable housing.

The CHAIRMAN. Thank you, Senator Heitkamp.

We will now hear from our witnesses. I want to remind each of the witnesses that your full testimony will be made a part of the official hearing record. Please keep your statements to five minutes so that we may have time for questions.

We look forward to hearing the testimony beginning with Chairwoman Diver. Please proceed.

STATEMENT OF HON. KAREN DIVER, CHAIRWOMAN, FOND DU LAC BAND OF LAKE SUPERIOR CHIPPEWA INDIANS

Ms. DIVER. Good afternoon. Thank you so much for having me here today.

I am Karen Diver, Chairwoman of the Fond du Lac Band of Lake Superior Chippewa of Minnesota. I suppose it should be said Chippewa, Choctaw, and Cherokee. That reminds me of a really bad Country song or something.

I did provide some rather extensive written testimony. I think I would like to expand on that written testimony just a bid.

No doubt we have challenges in Indian Country regarding housing. Many of you have already noted those, very lengthy waiting lists. Just when we do a project and think we have made some statistical impact on it, another generation comes along or more people become eligible or want to move home.

Overcrowding and homelessness, we all know that at the McKinney-Vento definition of homelessness does not work in Indian Country because it does not take into account couch surfing and overcrowded conditions. That is what homelessness looks like in Indian Country.

The age of our housing stock, as also noted, '37 Act housing, in many cases, was built substandard and now it is further stressed by overcrowding. Additionally, there are more restrictions on that housing not enabling us to convert them from rentals to NAHASDA homeownerships because you lose crucial maintenance monies that are restricted to '37 Act housing.

At some point, kind of fixing the incongruity between '37 Act housing and NAHASDA housing and allowing us to be entrepreneurial and self determined with that older housing stock would be something that would be very useful to tribes in meeting these new needs. Development challenges were noted, everything from loss of land base, the very rural nature of our housing development, infrastructure development, the difficulty in using different sources of funding; sometimes for development, if we would like to use Indian Health Service dollars, USDA dollars combined with NAHASDA dollars, BIA road money.

Some of those barriers were removed during the period of the ARRA funding but now back in regular funding cycles. A lot of those restrictions remain in place and do not allow us to leverage within existing housing funding sources for development.

All of the challenges being duly noted, we should actually look at the opportunities. There are vast numbers of opportunities. Minnesota conducts a homeless count every three years in Minnesota. When asked what does homelessness look like on reservations, they never counted homelessness on reservations, yet that was the tool they used to deploy resources in Minnesota for State housing funds.

Tribal entities worked with the State to conduct the first ever tribal homeless counts in Minnesota. That resulted in the State doing three years of extraordinary funding to Indian Country to make up for the many years of deficits.

We were able to use those funds and leverage it with other sources much like any other housing developer and operator that would operate in any municipality or county. Federal Home Loan Bank funds and other sources were brought to the table and leveraged our NAHASDA dollars about 6 to 1 for every dollar of NAHASDA money, six dollars in other matching funds.

Twenty-four units supportive of housing to help a chronic and long-term homeless population on the reservation. Not only are we providing them with the housing first model, but we are providing them with those services which allow them to become self-sufficient over the long term and hopefully move into regular housing without supportive services.

We have seen families where this is the first time in their families lives their children have been able to stay in the same school for three to four years in a row for the first time in their life. You cannot count the amount that helps in remedial actions and other services that would be necessary for those children.

Flexibility for new housing models beyond rentals and homeowners is critical for NAHASDA. The VASH vouchers, thank you all of you who helped us make tribes eligible for VASH vouchers, meeting a critical need for our veterans. That should be hitting fairly soon. We offered commentary to make sure we can serve those folks as best we can with those supportive services.

Tribes are being trained on new models of housing consistent with the continuums of care, everything from emergency rental assistance to down payment assistance. We offer those things but just so you know, once we do, those funds are no longer available to do housing development out of NAHASDA.

We can be entrepreneurial with a little bit more. We have the self-governance and program capabilities. We need your help to get those resources so we can offer as many alternatives as possible for our home community.

With that, I thank you.

[The prepared statement of Ms. Diver follows:]

PREPARED STATEMENT OF HON. KAREN DIVER, CHAIRWOMAN, FOND DU LAC BAND OF LAKE SUPERIOR CHIPPEWA INDIANS

Mr. Chairman, members of the Committee, I am Karen R. Diver, Chairwoman of the Fond du Lac Band of Lake Superior Chippewa. On behalf of the Band, I would like to thank you for holding this hearing on S. 710 to reauthorize the Native American Housing Assistance and Self-Determination Act.

NAHASDA is an invaluable tool to help tribes meet the longstanding and very serious lack of affordable housing in Indian country. We very much appreciate all of the work that this Committee has done, and continues to do, to reauthorize this important legislation.

The Unmet Need for Decent, Safe and Affordable Housing in Indian Country

As this Committee knows from your work on this matter, the housing needs for Native Americans are substantial. Native Americans continue to suffer from the most substandard housing compared to the population at large. The Fond du Lac Band, like tribes nationwide, has longstanding and severe housing needs. At Fond du Lac we have been striving to combat the endemic problems that result from the lack of a sufficient supply of decent, safe and affordable housing. NAHASDA has been critical to our ability to begin to make progress in addressing those needs, but there is still much to do.

The Fond du Lac Band occupies a small reservation in northeastern Minnesota. The Band has approximately 4,200 members, and we provide health, education, social services, public safety, housing and other governmental services to more than 6,700 Indian people who live on or near our Reservation.

The lack of safe and affordable housing has been a serious problem for the Fond du Lac Band for decades. In working to address this, we face several considerable challenges.

One such challenge is our land base. Although our Reservation encompasses 100,000 acres, the federal allotment policy of the 1880s left us with the poorest lands; our most valuable lands went to timber companies and homesteaders. In addition, our Reservation is located in a geographic area that contains mostly marginal lands that require costly drainage projects for the land to be useable. Our lands are considered a difficult environment for affordable housing because they require high development costs associated with substandard soils, expensive sewage systems, and a lack of decent infrastructure. In an effort to meet our members' housing needs, we have to invest significant funds to remediate our Reservation lands, purchase other lands, and construct the infrastructure (septic systems, water and sewer lines, roads, and utility services) that is essential to provide housing.

A second challenge we face has been, and continues to be, the very substantial need among our members for affordable housing. Although we have made strides in expanding economic and employment opportunities on our reservation, poverty and unemployment persist. According to the 2010 Census, 11.6 percent of Minnesotans were living in poverty while the poverty rate among American Indians in the State was 39.5 percent. And in 2010, the median household income for American Indians in Minnesota was approximately $27,000, which was less than half the statewide median of $55,459.[1] As to unemployment, according to the U.S. Census

---

[1] *See* Minnesota Council of Nonprofits, *Minnesota Budget Project.*

Bureau American Community Survey 2006–2010, unemployment at Fond du Lac was 14.1 percent, while unemployment among all Minnesotans was less than half that—at 6.4 percent. The large number of Indian people who are unemployed or living below the poverty level puts a huge demand on tribes to provide affordable housing.

A third challenge we face is a very limited housing stock, and limited financial resources to build, acquire and maintain a supply of housing sufficient to meet the needs of our members. Many of our housing units are over twenty years old, with the oldest units built more than 40 years ago, in 1970. Because of the age of our housing stock, the units are constantly in need of maintenance and repairs. Approximately 30 percent of our housing units require major renovation, such as the replacement of roofs and siding, as well as upgrades in plumbing and other utility systems, and the replacement of windows and doors. Other units require routine repairs and maintenance, the average cost of which currently is $11,000.

Our current housing stock is simply not sufficient to meet the need for low income housing. Because of the costs of maintenance and repair, we have little left to acquire or build additional low income rental units. We currently have a waiting list of 185 applicants seeking low income and homeownership housing. We have many other tribal members who are also in need of housing, but who do not apply and therefore do not appear on our waiting list—either because they feel that the wait for housing is too long, or because they believe that they might not meet the income eligibility requirements for low income housing. Accordingly, our waiting list understates the full need for housing among our members.

The severity of our housing shortage also means that many Indian households that we serve—close to 20 percent of our service population—live in overcrowded homes. It is not uncommon on our Reservation and among our people to find 10 or more individuals living together in a two-bedroom home. Overcrowding, in turn, accelerates the wear and tear on those homes, creating a vicious cycle of need. Overcrowded housing creates other risks. It increases the risk of fire and accidents. It can lead to unsanitary conditions, with increased spreading of normally preventable illnesses. Overcrowded housing also leads to a stressful environment that can create or exacerbate family dysfunction. Overcrowded homes can be especially harmful to children, putting at risk their health, development, and educational success.

Overcrowded housing is also a symptom of a larger housing problem—homelessness and near-homelessness. Many people in overcrowded homes are either actually homeless or only a step away from becoming homeless, but these individuals are often overlooked in the traditional means by which homelessness is counted. The standard procedure for estimating homelessness is through point-in-time counts of the number of persons who, on a given night, are living either in a shelter or on the street. This approach makes sense in urban areas where shelters are available or homelessness is visible, but does not fit in rural communities (or Indian country) where small populations are dispersed over a larger geographic area, and emergency shelters are uncommon. As discussed in a number of studies, including a 2013 report by the Housing Assistance Council (HAC) and the Corporation for Supportive Housing (CSH),[2] in rural communities (including Indian county), homeless individuals and families "typically experience precarious housing conditions, moving from one extremely substandard, overcrowded housing situation to another, often doubling or tripling up with friends or relatives." As the HAC and CSH further found, these problems are compounded in Indian country, which has experienced a history of persistent poverty and inadequate housing on tribal lands.

The severity of homelessness among Indian communities was confirmed by a series of studies of homelessness among Native Americans on Reservations in Minnesota, including the Fond du Lac Reservation. As those reports explained:[3]

> The federal definition of homelessness does not include doubling up with family and friends, and so tells only part of the story in describing the experience of homelessness on Indian reservations. On reservations extended family ties are strong, and traditions dictate that those who have housing will take in those who do not, if at all possible.

> Doubling up with family or friends is often the last housing arrangement a person has before becoming literally homeless, and it is common for people to go back and forth between doubling up and homelessness.

---

[2] Housing Assistance Council and Corporation for Supportive Housing, *Conducting Homeless Counts on Native American Lands: A Toolkit* (February 2013).
[3] Wilder Research, *2006 Study: Homeless and Near-Homeless People on Northern Minnesota Indian Reservations,* at 2 (Nov 2007).

These studies further found that a disproportionately high number of Native Americans in Minnesota are homeless. A study done in 2012 found that although Native American adults are only 1 percent of the State population, they are 10 percent of the adults identified as homeless. And while Native American youth (under age 21) are only 2 percent of the youth population in Minnesota, they are 22 percent of the homeless youth that are unaccompanied by an adult. [4]

Why NAHASDA Is Critical to Helping Address Unmet Housing Needs in Indian Country

The Fond du Lac Band—like many tribes across the Nation—is doing everything it can to address these serious housing needs. The resources provided through NAHASDA have been critical to this effort.

At the most basic level, NAHASDA has been key to our ability to repair and maintain our existing housing stock. We have also relied on NAHASDA to address the costs of infrastructure—especially septic and water systems—needed for housing. We also use a small part of our NAHASDA funds to aid eligible Band members with emergency rental assistance.

But in addition, as a result of the funds provided through NAHASDA, the Fond du Lac Band has been able to use a portion of those funds, supplemented by other Band resources, to partner with state and private entities in an effort to begin to more comprehensively address housing needs. In particular, in July 2010, we completed construction of 24 units of Supportive Housing to provide housing and related social services to low income tribal members and their families who are homeless or live in overcrowded conditions or places that are unfit for habitation. The project was constructed using a combination of funding sources that included NAHSADA, tribal, private non-profits, and state funds. This housing development includes a mix of housing types to meet a range of needs—with several townhomes for families, as well as an apartment building with efficiency, one and two-bedroom units. We used green technology to reduce long-term operating expenses. Our Housing Division operates these supportive housing units in conjunction with our Human Services Division so that social and related services are also provided to these tenants to address the barriers to their ability to maintain housing and to create a support system to prevent homelessness. These supportive services are provided both on-site and within walking distance of the housing units.

In July 2013, the Band, again in partnership with state, private and non-profit entities, was able to leverage tribal and NAHASDA funds to complete construction of the first Veteran's Supportive Housing facility in Indian country. Our Veterans Supportive Housing consists of 10 units to provide housing for Native American Veterans and their families who are homeless or at risk of homelessness. Because these units are operated as supportive housing, our Social Services Division works with the Veterans who are tenants in these units to provide medical and social services to help them address problems that put them at risk of homelessness. In short, we seek to provide them with an affordable, stable home and the tools to gain more control over the decisions that affect their lives.

We are grateful to the members of this Committee for the work done last December to have Congress include, in the FY15 Omnibus Appropriations Act, a provision that authorizes the Department of Housing and Urban Development to set aside a portion of the funds provided for the HUD-Veterans Supportive Housing Program (HUD–VASH), for use in tribally-administered housing projects to serve Native American veterans. As many of you know, by the HUD–VASH program, HUD and the Department of Veterans Affairs work to combat homelessness among veterans by providing vouchers so that they can obtain rental assistance for housing along with related supportive counseling and clinical services. The program, revived by President Bush in 2008 and supported by President Obama, has been very successful, as HUD's data shows a 17 percent reduction in homelessness among veterans from 2009 to 2012. But due to an oversight in the law, the HUD–VASH program had not been available to Native American veterans for use in tribally-administered housing projects. The provisions that you and your colleagues included in the FY15 Omnibus Appropriations Act established the first critical step to fixing this problem. We understand that HUD is now working on regulations to implement the Tribal VASH program, and the availability of HUD–VASH vouchers for use in tribally-administered Veteran's Supportive Housing will be of tremendous assistance by providing us, and other tribes, with help on the operating subsidy that is essential to our ability to effectively provide supportive housing to veterans.

---

[4] Wilder Research, *2012 Minnesota Homeless Study: Fact Sheet, Initial Findings, Characteristics and Trends,* at 2 (April 2013).

The Reauthorization Bill, S. 710

We support S. 710. We agree with its provisions, set out in section 102 of the bill, to help streamline the environmental review process required for housing construction and rehabilitation. This is especially important since tribes, like Fond du Lac, often rely on a variety of funding sources from different agencies to build housing and should not be subject to multiple and potentially different NEPA requirements for the same project.

We also support the provisions of S. 710 which would not cap appropriations at the current funding level but would instead allow the appropriators to adjust funding levels to meet need.

In addition, we very strongly support section 501 of the bill, which would permanently authorize the Tribal HUD–VASH program that was initiated in the FY15 Omnibus Appropriations Act. The rules set out in that section will allow the program to be implemented within the framework established by NAHASDA, which should ensure that the program fits the unique needs for veterans supportive housing in Indian country.

Housing represents the single largest expenditure for most Indian families. The development of housing has a major impact on the national economy and the economic growth and health of regions and communities. Housing is inextricably linked to access to jobs and healthy communities and the social behavior of the families who occupy it. The failure to achieve adequate housing leads to significant societal costs.

Decent, affordable, and accessible housing fosters self-sufficiency, brings stability to families, vitality to distressed communities, and supports overall economic growth. In particular, it improves life outcomes for children. In the process, it reduces a host of costly social and economic problems that place enormous strains on the education, public health, social service, law enforcement, criminal justice, and welfare systems.

As illustrated by the Fond du Lac Band's experience, NAHASDA is critical not only to our ability to maintain existing affordable housing for our members—but also to our ability to leverage federal and tribal funds into innovative partnerships with the state and private sector so that we can expand the resources available to meet unmet housing needs. We have begun to make inroads on these challenges, but much remains to be done. NAHASDA is an essential tool for us to continue this important work, and we urge it be reauthorized on the terms set out in S. 710.

Miigwech. Thank you.

The CHAIRMAN. Thank you so much.

Mr. COOPER.

STATEMENT OF GARY COOPER, CHAIRMAN, LEGISLATIVE COMMITTEE, NATIONAL AMERICAN INDIAN HOUSING COUNCIL

Mr. COOPER. Good afternoon.

Thank you, Mr. Chairman and members of the Committee.

My name is Gary Cooper. I am an enrolled member of the Cherokee Nation. I am Executive Director of the Housing Authority of the Cherokee Nation and I am Chairman of the Legislative Committee of the National American Indian Housing Council. I am here today in that role as Chairman of NAIHC's Legislative Committee. Thank you for the opportunity to appear.

NAIHC was founded in 1974 and for decades has provided invaluable training and technical assistance and other services to all tribes and tribal housing entities. The membership of NAIHC is expansive. We are comprised of 274 members representing 473 tribes and tribal housing organizations. NAIHC's members span the entire country from Florida to Alaska, from New Mexico to Maine and reside in each every State represented by the members of this Committee.

Our members are deeply appreciative of the consistent leadership this Committee provides to Congress related to the issues affecting tribal communities and tribal housing.

It comes as no surprise to you that tribal communities suffer the highest unemployment and poverty rates, the worst health, poor education options and the most substandard housing in Indian Country.

Native Americans disproportionately experience socio-economic challenges including high unemployment and extreme poverty that impact housing conditions in Indian Country. While Indian Country has made real strides in economic growth and development in the last 30 years, the sad truth is in 2015, poverty in America continues to have an Indian face.

Prior to the passage of NAHASDA in 1999, the model for all housing in Indian Country was pretty much a cookie cutter model that was the same whether it was Karen's region, my region or anywhere else. That does not work.

The passage of the Native American Housing Assistance and Self Determination Act of 1996 signaled a shift in that relationship between Federal and tribal governments with respect to housing programs. It also put decision-making at the local levels with the tribes under the self-determination part and recognized tribal sovereignty. It worked to improve housing conditions throughout Indian Country. By enacting it, it really helped to address the housing crisis that exists.

In preparation for NAHASDA being reauthorized this year, NAIHC began a vast outreach of our membership leading up to this point. We facilitated in-depth and ongoing discussions to look at the effectiveness of the Act, reviewed each of the individual components, rules and regulations and so on.

We reached out to our members and came up with some draft language that we would propose. We are happy to see that a number of those provisions are included in S. 710. We agree with the provisions contained in Section 101. This change will result in more efficient use of scarce Federal dollars.

We also strongly endorse the proposed changes to redundant environmental review requirements as provided in Section 102 of the bill. Our membership supports Section 201. We believe this provision aligns well with tribal sovereignty and self-determination in the delivery of Indian housing programs. We agree with Section 202, in binding commitments and useful life. We do not, as an organization, have a formal position on the bill language concerning un-dispersed funds.

Section 401 is also a section that is supported by our membership. As Chairwoman Diver mentioned, we are very ecstatic and enthusiastic to see HUD–VASH included in the bill so we can deliver much needed housing assistance to our Native American veterans. We look forward to the day that we can do that.

NAIHC does have some concerns with Section 503 of the bill. Our members do not support a chance to delivery of training and technical assistance from the way it has been in the past.

All in all, we support the remainder of the bill. We are happy with and support Sections 701, 702, 703, 704 and 705. We think this is a very good bill.

Thank you, Mr. Chairman, for your leadership on this important issue and for your kind invitation for us to appear today.

[The prepared statement of Mr. Cooper follows:]

PREPARED STATEMENT OF GARY COOPER, CHAIRMAN, LEGISLATIVE COMMITTEE, NATIONAL AMERICAN INDIAN HOUSING COUNCIL

Good Afternoon. My name is Gary Cooper, and I am an enrolled member of the Cherokee Nation, Executive Director of the Housing Authority of the Cherokee Nation, and Chairman of the Legislative Committee of the National American Indian Housing Council (NAIHC). I am here today in my capacity as Chairman of the NAIHC's Legislative Committee.

The NAIHC's 267 members represent nearly 470 tribes and tribally- designated housing entities from across the United States. NAIHC was established 41 years ago and continues to provide vital training and technical assistance to increase the managerial and administrative capacity of tribal governments.

Thank you for the opportunity to appear before you today.

Background on the National American Indian Housing Council

The NAIHC was founded in 1974 and for four decades has provided invaluable Training and Technical Assistance (T&TA) to all tribes and tribal housing entities; provided information to Congress regarding the issues and challenges that tribes face in the many issues of housing, infrastructure, and community and economic development arenas; and worked with key federal agencies to address these important issues.

The membership of NAIHC is expansive, comprised of 274 members representing 473 [1] tribes and tribal housing organizations. NAIHC's member tribes span the entire country from Florida to Alaska, from New Mexico to Maine and reside in each and every state represented by the Members of this Committee. Our members are deeply appreciative of the consistent leadership this Committee provides in Congress related to issues affecting tribal communities.

NAIHC's primary mission is to support tribal housing entities in their efforts to provide safe, decent, affordable, and culturally appropriate housing for Native people.

Profile of Indian Country in 2015

There are 566 federally-recognized Indian tribes in the United States. Tribal communities suffer the highest unemployment and poverty rates, the worst health, poor education options, and the most substandard housing in the country. Historically, Native Americans in the United States have faced worse housing conditions than other groups. Native Americans disproportionately experience socioeconomic challenges, including high unemployment and extreme poverty that impact housing conditions on Indian reservations and in other Indian areas.

The U.S. Census Bureau reported in 2013 that American Indians and Alaska Natives were almost twice as likely to live in poverty as the rest of the population— 27 percent compared with 14.3 percent. Over 40 percent of Native Americans in North Dakota and South Dakota live below the poverty line, and in seven other states (Arizona, Maine, Minnesota, Montana, Nebraska, New Mexico, and Utah) Native American poverty rates are about 30 percent or more. In addition, overcrowding, substandard housing, and homelessness are far more common in Native American communities. According to Census 2005–2009 American Community Survey data, 5.3 percent of homes on Native American lands lacked complete plumbing and 4.8 percent lacked complete kitchens. The comparable nationwide figures were 0.5 and 0.7 percent, respectively.

While Indian Country has made real strides in economic growth and development in the last 30 years, the sad truth is that in 2015, poverty in America continues to have an Indian face.

Federal Housing Programs Before 1996

Up to 1996, HUD dominated the design and implementation of housing programs in Indian Country. Funding and programs mirrored the 1937 Housing Act. Older

---

[1] There are 566 federally recognized Indian tribes and Alaska Native villages in the United States, all of which are eligible for membership in NAIHC. Other NAIHC members include state-recognized tribes eligible for housing assistance under the 1937 Housing Act and that were subsequently grandfathered in the Native American Housing Assistance and Self-Determination Act of 1996, and the Department of Hawaiian Home Lands, the state agency that administers the Native Hawaiian Housing Block Grant program.

housing developments on reservations are often called "cookie cutter," because the nature of the program did not contemplate cultural considerations and innovation in design.

Passage of the Native American Housing Assistance and Self-Determination Act (NAHASDA) in 1996 signaled a shift in the relationship between federal and tribal governments with respect to housing programs. NAHASDA is based on tribal decisionmaking at the local level and has resulted in improved housing conditions throughout Indian Country.

In enacting NAHASDA, Congress moved to address the housing crisis in Indian Country by consolidating federal housing programs into a single block grant made directly to Indian tribes or their tribally-designated housing entities (TDHEs).

For over 18 years, NAHASDA has been the cornerstone for providing housing assistance to low-income families on Indian reservations, in Alaska Native villages, and on Hawaiian Home Lands.

Essential Input on NAHASDA Reauthorization from Practitioners

Throughout 2012–2013, NAIHC held a series of outreach meetings to gather input from tribal leaders, Indian housing professionals and advocates for consideration during reauthorization deliberations on Capitol Hill. NAIHC's input relied heavily on individuals working in tribal housing management who possess the extensive experience necessary to assess NAHASDA's original intent and to take the lead in discussions on best practices and barriers (within NAHASDA) that Indian housing directors face on a regular basis.

The outreach facilitated in-depth, ongoing discussions to assess the effectiveness of the Act, its individual components, and its rules and regulations in meeting its intended purpose(s). The objective of this extensive outreach process was to have a reauthorized Act that more effectively accomplishes its objectives.

Input from this year-long process was catalogued and developed into a consensus reauthorization bill. NAIHC maintained regular communication with Members of Congress and staff throughout this process and shared copies of provisions and reasoning for those provisions in draft legislative language. In summary, NAIHC's proposed NAHASDA reauthorization is designed to strengthen tribal self-determination and remove agency-created barriers by establishing timelines for departmental approvals and streamlining administrative processes.

Comments on S. 710, NAHASDA Amendments of 2015

Title I—Block Grants and Grant Requirements

We agree with the provision to exempt Davis-Bacon requirements contained in section 101 of the bill. Clarification that recipients satisfy federal labor requirements when they apply tribally-adopted prevailing wage rates to all federal funding sources on projects funded all or in part by IHBG would result in additional relief from the burdens of the Davis-Bacon Act and will result in more efficient use of scarce federal dollars.

We also strongly endorse proposed changes to redundant environmental review requirements as provided in section 102 of the bill. These changes would provide recipients a streamlined process by applying a single environmental review carried out under NAHASDA that would satisfy all other applicable environmental review requirements, and in the process substantially reducing the administrative requirements to recipients. This provision would reduce delays and allow limited resources to be used elsewhere.

Title II—Affordable Housing Activities

NAIHC membership strongly supports section 201 to clarify that the Act's minimum rent requirement does not apply if a block grant recipient has a written policy governing rents or homebuyer payments charged for housing units. We understand some in the Senate may oppose this proposal, but these suggested amendments align well with tribal sovereignty and self-determination in the delivery of Indian housing programs.

We agree with section 202 to exempt subsequent homebuyers from binding commitments for the remaining useful life of the property. Many recipients feel the current regulations do not comport with the goals or intent of NAHASDA.

Section 202 that also relates to binding commitments and useful life agreements and would render them inapplicable if the aggregate value of improvement is less than 10,000 in a 5-year period.

While we support this construct, we believe a better approach would be to have binding commitments for the remaining useful life of the property not apply to improvements of privately owned homes if the cost of such improvements do not exceed 10 percent of the maximum total development cost for such home.

NAIHC supports section 202 which permits households participating in low-income rental unit to purchase through a contract to purchase, without re-qualifying, provided the household was low-income at the time of initial occupancy. Many feel the current regulations deter success in tenant employment opportunities.

Section 205 to increase Total Development Costs (TDC) to 20 percent. TDC is a general guide published by HUD based on a moderately designed house, and are determined by averaging the current construction costs as listed in two nationally-recognized residential construction cost indices for publicly bid construction of a good and sound quality.

Title III—Allocation of Grant Amounts

NAIHC does not have a formal position on the bill language related to undisbursed funds.

Title IV—Compliance, Audits, and Reports

Section 401 is a proposal that has been endorsed by NAIHC membership.

Title V—Other Housing Assistance for Native Americans

Section 501 of the bill would authorize the Secretary to establish a rental assistance program for Native American veterans modeled on the HUD—Veterans Affairs Supportive Housing (HUD–VASH) program. NAIHC *enthusiastically* supports this language.

NAIHC has grave concerns with section 503, which would fundamentally re-structure section 703 of NAHASDA relating to Training and Technical Assistance (T&TA). As proposed, section 503 would route T&TA through the department's Transformation Initiative, and would ensconce a competitive funding process in the authorizing statute. Further, it would render T&TA funds to an open competition involving national, regional, and for-profit organizations.

This is a major departure from the current delivery of T&TA outlined in statute. For many years, Indian tribes have volunteered to ''shave'' their respective block grant allocations and have the NAIHC use the funds to provide quality and relevant T&TA. Section 703 reflects this sentiment in providing that all authorized T&TA funds should be provided ''for a national organization representing Native American housing interests.'' Since NAHASDA's enactment in 1996, this language—and the resulting arrangement for the provision of T&TA—has not been challenged.

If the Committee seeks to acknowledge and further Indian self-determination and respect tribal sovereignty, it should affirm the language of section 703.

Title VII—Miscellaneous

NAIHC endorses section 701 the proposed language clarifying tribal housing programs may qualify as Community Based Development Organizations for the ICDBG program. NAIHC would urge language be added to specifically note that tribes and/or their Tribally Designated Housing Entity may also participate in Community Based Organizations.

NAIHC supports section 702 in the bill to repeal Section 801 of NAHASDA, relating to the limitation on the use of funds for the Cherokee Nation.

We also support provisions in the bill to reauthorize the Native Hawaiian Homeownership Act (sections 703 and 704). While we recognize there is hardened opposition to these provisions in the Senate, we stand by to assist in any way.

Finally, NAIHC supports section 705 in the bill regarding matching or cost-participation requirements, and section 706 regarding funding for methamphetamine clean-up projects.

While S. 710 is a very good offering and we would like to support this measure, we cannot in good faith do so as long as the T&TA provisions remain as they are. The current language eliminates section 703 entirely. Section 703 was included at the request of tribes so the NAIHC could provide much need training and technical assistance to tribal members. During the numerous amendment and reauthorization processes, tribes have not suggested amending or deleting section 703—ever.

NAIHC would be very happy to work with the Committee to find an alternative to the current T&TA provision. Thank you, Mr. Chairman for your leadership on this important matter and for your kind invitation to appear before you today

The CHAIRMAN. Thank you very much, Mr. Cooper.

Mr. SOSSAMON.

STATEMENT OF RUSSELL SOSSAMON, EXECUTIVE DIRECTOR, CHOCTAW NATION OF OKLAHOMA HOUSING AUTHORITY

Mr. SOSSAMON. Thank you, Mr. Chairman, Mr. Lankford, the last Senator from the great State of Oklahoma, Senator Heitkamp, and Senator Franken for your commitment and hard work to assist us in Indian Country, particularly in regard to housing.

I appreciate the opportunity to come and testify before this Committee. I have served as Executive Director of the Housing Authority of the Choctaw Nation of Oklahoma for the past 19 years.

To sum up my testimony today, I would say we need to reauthorize NAHASDA this year, preserve the included provisions that significantly increase our ability to be more effective and efficient in the delivery of our services, and refine the mechanism of the provision that incentivizes timely drawdown of funds from the HUD credit control system.

As Senator Heitkamp pointed out, you are all familiar with the severe conditions of housing in Indian Country, so I will not go into those needs right now. I will focus primarily on the benefits that NAHASDA has given the Choctaw Nation of Oklahoma the opportunity to create.

We created a 501(c)(3) home finance corporation that is a CDFI to address the homeownership needs of our tribal members. This corporation provides direct lending as well as leverage lending through private lending partners.

To date, we have made over $45 million worth of direct loans. We manage a portfolio valued at over $22 million which consists of 650 mortgages. Annually, we do approximately 100 direct loans. We leverage another 84 loans through our lending partners, not just in our service area, but across the United States wherever tribal members live. To date, we have leveraged over $70 million worth of funds for mortgage lending.

Along with the mortgage lending, we provide home buyer and financial counseling. We focus, not only on what it is going to take to be a successful homeowner but how to use your home as an asset throughout your life to achieve other goals.

We would like to thank Chairman Barrasso and his staff for including in the bill the treatment of the program income, to clarify that so that we do not have to track those virtually in perpetuity which wastes resources that could be otherwise focused on serving our housing needs.

Senator Heitkamp pointed out that we are going to have to come up with a different type of strategy. I believe Section 502, the 99 year leasehold, will create an environment where homeowners will invest on trust land and it will attract private capital, not only meeting housing needs but also hopefully expanding and creating economies on those lands.

Section 705, the leveraging provision, I believe will be a part of that strategy. It will be comprehensive and it will take numerous angles and approaches to solve these problems. We have to look at how we address these differently than we have ever looked at them in the past. The environment has changed. We have to work together, the Federal Government, the State governments, the tribes, and our people.

One of the things that we are in the process of developing is a new concept of leveraging the other services in coordination within. We will work with our tribal members to help them actually move beyond depending on us to support them in their housing needs, to get them to a point where they can meet their own housing needs.

We have to do that working with higher education and career development, as well as economic development in the area so there will be good jobs they will need to be able to afford housing. That is a big piece that has been absent.

I thank you for this opportunity. I thank you for introducing S. 710 and working for the reauthorization of NAHASDA. I would be happy to answer any questions.

[The prepared statement of Mr. Sossamon follows:]

PREPARED STATEMENT OF RUSSELL SOSSAMON, EXECUTIVE DIRECTOR, CHOCTAW NATION OF OKLAHOMA HOUSING AUTHORITY

I. Introduction

Good morning Chairman Barrasso, Vice Chairman Tester, and distinguished members of the United States Senate Committee on Indian Affairs (SCIA). My name is Russell Sossamon. I am an enrolled member of the Choctaw Nation of Oklahoma (CNO) and for the past nineteen (19) years have served as the Executive Director of the Housing Authority of the Choctaw Nation of Oklahoma (HACNO), located in Hugo, Oklahoma. It is an honor to be invited here to present testimony on behalf of the Choctaw Nation of Oklahoma.

I want to thank the Committee for holding this important legislative hearing this afternoon on S. 710, The Native American Housing Assistance and Self-Determination Reauthorization Act of 2015 (NAHASDA). And I in particular want to express my sincere appreciation to Chairman Barrasso and his staff for introducing last week the bill for which this hearing is being conducted as the vehicle to move NAHASDA reauthorization towards passage in the Senate. As a long-time official at the CNO working in all areas of the tribal housing, I am professionally enthused by seeing this movement on Capitol Hill so quickly on this much-needed legislation barely 2 months into this new 114th Congress. And I am personally heartened not only by the good intentions that brought the bill forward but also by the good that I know will result in my community at the CNO and throughout Indian Country once the legislation is enacted. I am confident that Senator Barrasso and his colleagues on the Committee will work to move the legislation without undue delay and I thank you all in advance for your hard work in doing so.

As you may know, I testified before this Committee in the last Congress nearly 2 years ago at an oversight hearing on "Identifying Barriers to Indian Housing Development and Finding Solutions." That was just a few months prior to the expiration of the most recent authorization of the NAHASDA at the end of FY 2013. Since that expiration over a year and a half ago, several bills have been introduced to reauthorize the NAHASDA in the Senate and House. Even prior to the expiration, the CNO, as a member of the National American Indian Housing Council (NAIHC) representing over 460 tribes and tribally-designated housing entities (TDHEs), worked with its fellow NAIHC members to push for the enactment of reauthorization legislation based upon the NAIHC's consensus-based draft bill recommendation. At the close of the last Congress, we came close but simply ran out of time. This speedy introduction of a reauthorization bill in this new Congress here in the Senate, as well as Rep. Steve Pearce's bill H.R. 360 introduced in the House earlier this year, should give enough time in the legislative process to enable all relevant issues to be raised and concerns to be addressed. If there is anything I can do after today's hearing to help ensure the current lapse in authorization is soon brought to an end by the enactment of reauthorization legislation, please let me know. I would be happy to assist in any way that I can.

In my testimony today, I will touch briefly upon a few of the provisions of Chairman Barrasso's bill that I believe will be particularly beneficial to the CNO and other tribes and TDHEs throughout Indian Country. One of those provisions is Section 705, pertaining to leveraging of NAHASDA funds, by enabling their use for matching or cost participation requirements under other federal and non-federal programs creating the potential to significantly assist the CNO and other NAHASDA recipients in multiplying the number of low-income tribal members we serve. The use of leveraging is a hallmark of the CNO's housing programs, and I therefore will share some of our beneficial programs and outcomes made possible by the NAHASDA and other federal funds, many of which have successfully used leveraging for years.

I will also lay out some background on the CNO and the challenges it faces in providing services to its members, as well as to members of dozens of other tribes who live within our Nation's service area. I will then examine some of the reasons why the provision of safe, quality, affordable housing in Indian Country generally, and within the CNO in particular, is such a challenge. This will be followed by background information on the federal legislative and administrative efforts to address that challenge, which ultimately culminated in the passage of the NAHASDA. That will lead me into examples of the innovative and effective housing programs administered through the HACNO, including the use of leveraging, to show why this Congress should continue to support tribal housing programs and work to quickly approve the reauthorization of the NAHASDA during this current fiscal year. Importantly, that reauthorization should include, as Senator Barrasso's bill currently does, the affirmation and respect for the negotiated-rulemaking process. Like all federal legislation that aims to accommodate the needs of many tribes across the country, from the perspective of a practitioner, there are some minor points in Senator Barrasso's bill that could be refined to increase its effectiveness, so in conclusion I will point out of those that Congress may consider examining for potential revision in the upcoming legislative process for the NAHASDA reauthorization.

II. Likely Benefits of S. 710, the Native American Housing Assistance and Self-Determination Reauthorization Act of 2015

The NAHASDA Reauthorization Act of 2015, if passed, would be a big stride in the federal government's fulfillment of its trust responsibility towards tribes and TDHEs. There are a multitude of benefits—the HUD–VASH program to assist homeless and at-risk veterans housing and with rental assistance programs; the elimination of redundant environmental reviews for multi-sourced federally funded projects; and the list goes on. I will touch upon a few of particular importance to the CNO and other NAHASDA recipients:

Section 101—Treatment of Program Income—Part of this section clarifies that income realized by a recipient from program income is "non-program income" that is not subject to restrictions on use. This is consistent with current regulations that are not as succinctly stated. The current regulations have to link together from various places for the intent to be clear. Often the those connections are not made and tribes are forced to use scarce resources on unnecessary administrative burdens. This will prevent recipients from having to track program income in perpetuity no matter how tenuous its connection to the original grant funds becomes over time.

Section 102—Environmental Review—This section eliminates excessive administrative burdens by providing tribes with a consistent single point of contact in conducting federal environmental review.

Section 103—Authorization of Appropriations—This provision's absence of a cap on the amount of authorized appropriations and permitting the option for the appropriation of such sums as may be necessary for the NAHASDA is much needed. While the NAHASDA funds are immensely appreciated by tribes and TDHEs and are tremendously helpful in beginning to meet tribal housing needs, they have never, in the history of the program, been sufficient to meet all of the basic housing needs of Indian tribes or to accomplish all of the purposes for which the NAHASDA was designed. Like many government programs, it is consistently and continuously underfunded. Therefore, tribes and their housing departments such as the HACNO have been forced to creatively think of ways to stretch their dollars and come up with unique and innovative tools to meet the housing needs in their communities. At the CNO, we are moving towards our goal of self-sufficiency, but still have a ways to go. We know the absence of any authorized funding cap is no guarantee of increased funding by appropriators, but it at least does not limit available options.

Section 202—Homeownership or Least-to-Own Low-Income Requirement and Income Targeting.

This provision removes requirements for binding commitments for de minimus home repairs and renovations. It will help the CNO address inefficiencies that have plagued our programs for years. Section 205(a)(2) of the NAHASDA requires that housing units remain affordable for either the remaining useful life of the property, as determined by the Secretary, or for another period that the Secretary determines is the longest feasible period of time consistent with sound economics and the purpose of the Act. The Act also requires that this affordability be secured through binding commitments satisfactory to the Secretary. Unfortunately these provisions regarding binding commitments have been interpreted so as to result in the unintended consequence of creating a lien on an entire housing unit and thereby bind up a much-needed housing asset, for even the smallest binding commitments that were made for very minor maintenance or repair expenditures. This creates an unnecessary expense and heavy administrative burden for small maintenance and repair expenditures. In short, Section 202 of the NAHASDA Reauthorization Act of 2015 would provide that the binding commitments for the remaining useful life of property will not apply to private home improvements if the costs of the improvements do not exceed 10 percent of the maximum total development cost for the home. Not only will this free up actual needed homes, but it will also permit us to use the monies currently spent on administering liens to actual programmatic use.

Section 501—HUD–VASH Program for Native American Veterans—This section provides opportunities for tribes to access resources to assist our homeless and at-risk veterans' housing and support needs. The rental vouchers in conjunction with coordinated support services of other vital programs and benefits allow us to go beyond fundamental housing and holistically meet the needs of our heroes.

Section 502—The 99-year Leasehold Interest in Trust or Restricted Lands for Housing Purposes—This provision will provide tribes and TDHEs with the ability to make long-term lease commitments that encourage potential homebuyers to invest and attract private capital that is desperately needed beyond currently available resources. This is a key condition to creating an environment that, in addition to enhancing our ability to achieve the primary objective of meeting housing needs, also has the potential to develop and/or expand economies into these areas.

Section 504—Loan Guarantees for Indian Housing—This section removes the cap on the total value of loans that the § 184 program can guarantee in a given year, thereby permitting the maximum usefulness of the program.

Section 701—Community-Based Organizations and Tribally Designated Housing Entities—This section would make TDHEs eligible as community-based development organizations (CBDOs) under the Indian Community Development Block Grant (ICDBG) program. This is particularly important to the CNO. Last year the CNO provided the matching funds for the ICDBG grant application for the HACNO to develop an Independent Elders Living Community development in a tribal area that currently does not have one. The project included the purchase of a minimum 20 acres of land, infrasture development of the property, and initial construction of 10 single family rental units. We have successfully completed six other projects just like this using the NAHSDA funding in the past in areas across half of our total service area. These initial sights were shovel ready and expanded when the American Recovery and Reinvestment Act (ARRA) funding was made available. Other funding has also been used to expand the existing sites. Now we are planning on developing similar sites across the other half of our service area over a five-year period. The only reason our application was not funded was because of the absence of a CBDO designation. While the NAHASDA legislation has improved over the years to adapt to changes in the environment to take advantage of opportunities and create solutions to our challenges, the ICDBG language remained constant, becoming obsolete at best and in our circumstance actually illogical. This measure is long overdue and tremendously needed.

Section 705—Leveraging—This provision will allow NAHASDA funds to be used as matching or cost participation funds under any other federal or non-federal program. As noted in more detail below, CNO's Home Finance Program already provides assistance through the leveraging of funds with lending partners to increase the number of potential home loans throughout the country. The Home Finance Program also has leveraged nearly $70,000,000 through participating lending partners who provide mortgages as part of government guarantee programs such as the Native American Section 184, Federal Housing Administration (FHA), Veterans Administration (VA), and U.S. Department of Agriculture Rural Development home loan programs. The Nation appreciates this opportunity to potentially use NAHASDA funds in more varied ways to multiply the results of our programs and services.

Before I delve into some of the success stories leveraging have enabled at the CNO, some background information on the Nation and its NAHASDA-funded programs is provided for context.

III. The Choctaw Nation of Oklahoma—Large-Scale Challenges and Opportunities

The housing issues in Indian Country cannot be separated from the big-picture social and economic challenges it also faces, and the CNO knows those challenges all too well. The CNO is the third largest Indian tribe in America, with over 200,000 enrolled tribal members spread all across the country. In a word, the CNO is immense. Inherent with that greater size and breadth are even greater responsibilities that are placed on the shoulders of the Nation's government to look after the welfare of its members. To add to that responsibility, the Nation's service area encompasses 10½ counties in southeastern Oklahoma, a land area larger than the entire state of Massachusetts, and within that service area are American Indian and Alaska Native constituents who may be far from their original tribal communities but to whom the CNO nonetheless provides services. Just one example is the tremendous demand placed on the Choctaw Nation of Oklahoma Health Services (CNOHS), which have provided healthcare services to patients who hailed from 148 different American Indian and Alaska Native tribal groups.

With an increasing tribal population and stifling economic conditions that have hit tribal communities such as the CNO particularly hard over the past several years, the social and economic needs of the Nation's and its members continue to grow. This increased need is particularly acute in the area of housing.

IV. The Housing Challenges in Indian Country and for the CNO

The challenges to providing quality, affordable housing in Indian Country generally and within the CNO specifically stem mostly from the broader overriding economic realities that occur in tribal communities. While the country in general has experienced an economic downturn and slow recovery over the past several years, this trend is greatly magnified in tribal communities. Often there is a lack of basic infrastructure and employment opportunities. These employment and infrastructure challenges exacerbate the housing situation in Indian Country. As countless other witnesses have testified at hearings such as this has historically been the case at the national level, Native Americans face some of the worst housing and living conditions in the country, and the availability of affordable, adequate, safe housing in Indian Country falls far below that of the general U.S. population.

The housing needs of members of the CNO, especially given the large size and breadth of its population, reflect the great need across Indian Country. However, because there are also many tribal members from other tribes across the country living within the CNO's service area, there are also unique challenges for the HACNO, as shown by the following figures for Fiscal Year 2015:

- Nearly seventeen percent (17 percent) of the American Indian/Alaska Native (AIAN) population living within the CNO's service are tribal members from other tribes.
- Approximately 10,628 households within the CNO's service area are considered low-income, meaning they have annual incomes of less than 80 percent of the national median annual income. Of those households, an astounding 29.7 percent earn only between 30 percent and 50 percent of the national median annual income, and even worse, 29.8 percent earn less than 30 percent of the national median annual income.
- Approximately 1,505 AIAN households within the CNO's service area are overcrowded or lack a kitchen or plumbing.
- Of the AIAN households within the CNO's service area, 2,086 households have a house cost burden greater than 50 percent of their annual income.
- In starkest terms, during this fiscal year the HACNO has a shortfall of 9,995 low-income units.

In sum, there is a severe housing shortage in our service area's tribal communities, resulting in overcrowded conditions. Many of the homes that do exist lack basic amenities that most Americans take for granted, such as full kitchens and plumbing, and even then many of the existing homes are in need of substantial repairs.

As shown by the low-income numbers above that persist within our tribal communities, the HACNO (and more generally, the CNO itself) understands that, in order to address acute housing needs, it is necessary to take a holistic approach that addresses the poverty cycle more generally to make our tribal members and other constituents that we serve self-sufficient—this is how we move from homelessness to homeownership. And that is why the HACNO views its mission from a higher level with two prongs, one to address the lack of affordable housing and the other to address the poverty cycle that produces and reinforces such a lack of housing. The CNO and its HACNO truly believe that, to paraphrase a metaphor, although it may be necessary in the short run to give a man a fish to eat today, it is better to teach him how to fish so that in the long run he can eat for a lifetime. In order to pay a mortgage and become a homeowner, a person first needs a job to earn income, and that requires education, training, and career development. Like the partnerships laid out below that we use to address home financing with a variety of loanassistance products, we likewise partner with other educational and social programs provided by the CNO as well as by the federal government and other local and tribal governments to build the whole person in a variety of ways. The support we provide through NAHASDA funding and related programs is one of the critical pieces to building that whole person.

V. Background on Indian Housing Legislation and Administration, Culminating with the Native American Housing Assistance and Self-Determination Act (NAHASDA)

Prior to the NAHASDA, housing assistance for Native American tribes and Alaska Natives was provided by various programs under the Housing Act of 1937 and other legislation. While these programs provided a broad range of assistance, they were administratively cumbersome and ineffective. They required separate applications and program administration, had different eligibility requirements, and were characterized by micro-management and detailed one-size-fitsall mandates. The programs were merely an extension of generic and often urban-oriented housing programs, failing to recognize the unique social, cultural, and economic needs of Native American communities.

In 1960, in the aftermath of the destruction of Indian homes in California by fire, the Bureau of Indian Affairs requested that the Department of Housing and Urban Development ("HUD") address Indian housing needs. In 1961, two major events changed the Indian housing landscape. First, the Public Housing Administration (PHA, HUD's predecessor) recognized tribal governments as local governing bodies that could establish Indian housing authorities (IHA) under tribal law by approving a tribal ordinance. Second, PHA also determined that states could establish IHAs in cases where a tribal government was not federally recognized but exercised all necessary powers. Soon after, the self-help or mutual help concept took hold and was based on the idea that a homebuyer would contribute land, material, or labor ("sweat equity") towards the purchase of a home. In December 1962, PHA announced the first mutual help housing program, and in 1964, the San Carlos Apache IHA launched the first mutual help project. Indian homes were developed under this program known as "Old Mutual Help" until 1976.

In the early 1970s, there were high expectations for the Federal Government to work with tribes and IHAs to satisfy national Indian housing goals and to address the reality of inadequate management systems. In 1971, the Government Accounting Office (GAO) issued a Congressional report on Indian housing that recommended a national Indian housing policy to stimulate agency coordination and accelerate the completion of projects. In 1984 HUD formally created the Office of Indian Housing (OIH) with its own staff to specifically oversee the development and management of Indian housing programs.

In 1990, Congress established the National Commission on American Indian, Alaska Native, and Native Hawaiian Housing, which two years later submitted to Congress a national blueprint plan for Indian housing. On October 1, 1993, the HUD Office of Indian Housing (OIH) at HUD Headquarters in Washington, D.C. and the Regional Office of Indian Programs (OIPs) became the Office of Native American Programs (ONAP).

In 1996, Congress passed the Native American Housing Assistance and Self-Determination Act ("NAHASDA") to provide federal statutory authority to address the above-mentioned housing disparities in Indian Country. The NAHASDA is the cornerstone for providing housing assistance to low-income Native American families on Indian reservations, in Alaska Native villages, and on native Hawaiian home lands. Since the passage of the NAHASDA in 1996 and its funding and implementation in 1998, the Indian Housing Block Grant (IHBG), the primary funding component of the NAHASDA, has been the single largest source of funding for housing for Native American communities and in Alaska Native villages. The NAHASDA also includes the Title VI loan guarantee program, which enables tribal members to more easily access home loans. Administered by HUD, the NAHASDA specifies a wide range of activities are that are eligible for funding. These activities include but are not limited to down-payment assistance, property acquisition, new construction, safety programs, planning and administration, and housing rehabilitation. Not only do IHBG funds support new housing development, acquisition, rehabilitation, and other housing services that are critical for tribal communities; they cover essential planning and operating expenses for tribal housing programs. A significant portion of IHBG funds are required for planning, administration, housing management, and services. Without this critical federal funding, many tribal housing authorities would be unable to operate.

While some members of Congress are now focusing on the unexpended funds in the NAHASDA block grant accounts, and mistakenly conclude that the program is overfunded. In fact, despite the positive developments in federal law and the impact of the NAHASDA, the funding it provides is plainly and simply insufficient to meet the existing and, in fact, growing housing need in our tribal communities.

VI. Innovations and Examples from the Housing Authority of the Choctaw Nation of Oklahoma

Out of sheer necessity and in the interest of promoting tribal self-determination and selfgovernance, tribes across the nation have begun developing innovative programs that complement the NAHASDA programs in order to meet the tremendous housing backlog in Indian Country. The HACNO has been at the forefront of these innovations in Indian Country, in order to address the housing needs not just of our members but of Native American tribal members from across the country.

a. United States Housing and Urban Development Section 184 Indian Home Loan Guarantee Program & NAHASDA Title VI Housing Activities Loan Guarantee Program

The Section 184 Loan Guarantee Program was created by the Housing and Community Development Act of 1992 to address the lack of mortgage lending in Indian Country. The HUD Section 184 program is a mortgage loan product designed to resemble a conventional, or private, housing loan program. There are no income limits for the Section 184 program. Local lenders become registered with the program and as such the federal government guarantees up to 100 percent of the home loans provided by such lenders to tribal members. Initially, the program gained acceptance in areas such as Oklahoma and Alaska, where much of the property in Indian areas has passed out of trust status and into "fee" status, meaning that the Federal Government no longer holds title to the individual parcel for the benefit of the tribe or the individual tribal member. Over time, the program has gained some traction on trust lands. Because the Section 184 Indian Home Loan program is guaranteed by the federal government, the program has provided much needed access to capital to many individual Natives that might otherwise find home financing difficult. The Section 184 program is the most successful Indian Country mortgage program. However, it should be noted that fewer than 20 percent of the Section 184 loans made to tribal members have been made on tribal trust or individual allotment land. More than half of the Section 184 loans have been made in Alaska and Oklahoma and because of the unique non-reservation system of land tenure for most Indian and Alaska Native groups in those states, nearly all of those loans were made for homes on fee simple land rather than trust land.

In addition to the Section 184 program, under Title VI of the NAHASDA, HUD is authorized to guarantee notes or other obligations issued by Indian tribes, or tribal housing entities, if approved by the tribe, for the purpose of financing affordable housing activities as described in Section 202 of the NAHASDA. Eligible borrowers must be a tribe or a tribal housing entity that is an IHBG program recipient. IHBG funds may be used as security for the guarantee or other obligation. The objectives of the program are to enhance the development of affordable housing activities, increase access to capital to further economic growth, and encourage the participation, in the financing of tribal housing programs, of financial institutions that do not normally serve tribal areas.

b. Choctaw Home Finance Services: On the Path from Self-Determination to Self-Sustainability through Nationwide Direct and Leveraged Home Lending in Indian Country

Tribes are increasingly exploring innovative ways to utilize the NAHASDA grant funds, combined with tribal funds and other resources, to maximize housing project outputs. The passage of the NAHASDA in 1996 and its funding in 1998, as well as other complementary Indian housing programs, have spurred the HACNO to creatively partner with lenders or utilize existing funds to enhance the effectiveness, efficiency, and success of housing projects. There is no greater example of such creativity in Indian Country than the HACNO's flagship program for home finance services offered through the Choctaw Home Finance Corporation.

The Choctaw Home Finance Corporation (CHFC) was incorporated in 2002 as a 501(c)(3) not-for-profit corporation to be the lending institution for the Choctaw Nation's Home Finance Program activities. The CHFC is also a certified Community Development Financial Institution (CDFI) through the U.S. Department of Treasury, meaning the federal government recognizes it as a financial institution working in underserved and economically-distressed markets that are often times not served by other traditional financial institutions. The CDFI certification enables the CHFC to access financial and technical award assistance through such things as the Native American CDFI Assistance Program, among others.

The CHFC is dedicated to successful private homeownership by offering affordable mortgage loans and counseling services to Native American families nationwide through its Home Finance Program, with a particular emphasis on serving low-income families who likely would not otherwise be able to own a home of their own. The Home Finance Program provides assistance through both direct lending as well as through the leveraging of funds with lending partners to increase the number of potential home loans throughout the country. (Leveraging funds is simply investing with borrowed money in a way that multiplies potential gains). The Home Finance Program has assisted not just members of the CNO but Native American families throughout Indian Country with over $45,000,000 in direct loans for home-ownership and down payment/closing cost assistance. The Home Finance Program also has leveraged just under $70,000,000 through participating lending partners who provide mortgages as part of government guarantee programs such as the Native American Section 184, Federal Housing Administration (FHA), Veterans Administration (VA), and U.S. Department of Agriculture Rural Development home loan programs. The private lending partners that CHFC has worked with include Wells Fargo, First United Bank, First Mortgage Company, First American Mortgage, Colonial Mortgage, Bank 2, Principal Mortgage Company, Arvest Bank, Gateway Mortgage, First Bank, BancFirst, Bank of Oklahoma, and Equity Bank.

The CHFC has a number of loan products available to meet the variety of financing needs of the families we serve. These products include loans for purchasing, refinancing, construction, improvements, and energy efficiency upgrades. One of these loan products, a direct loan to purchase a new home or refinance their current home at a more affordable rate and/or term, helps families receive an affordable loan with manageable fees. It also includes extremely professional guidance by a staff whose mission is to enhance the lives of all members through opportunities designed to develop healthy, successful and productive lifestyles.

Another loan product is a progressively subsidized homebuyer construction and finance service specifically for our low-income Native American families. The interest rate and terms are specific to low-income family needs, and the construction service is extremely valuable to those who need the added construction support from trained construction professionals to make informed decisions and get the most out of the amount they qualify for.

The CHFC also provides small, affordable streamline loans for home improvement, rehabilitation and/or energy efficiency upgrades. These loans help with necessary repairs to improve living conditions and property values, and also help with energy efficiency that results in lower utility payments, thereby freeing up more disposable income.

The CHFC closes on average 100 loans a year for Native American mortgages and down payment assistance. Additionally we leverage an average of 85 loans per year with our private lending partners. CHFC manages a loan portfolio of over $23,000,000.

The Home Finance Program is designed to function as a revolving loan fund. Funds are loaned out to the Native American participant and paid back in the form of principal and interest payments. The funds are then loaned back out to other Native American participants. There is a multiplier effect at work within the Program—the more loans made, the more principal and interest is repaid and those funds are then used to provide even more loans. This truly creates a self-sustaining service that sets the HACNO and its program participants on the path to self-sufficiency.

As a HUD-approved counseling agency, the CHFC also offers homeowner counseling services. Prior to extending a loan, each borrower is required to complete a homebuyer counseling session that provides education and information about the responsibilities and commitments required to be a successful homeowner. These sessions cover understanding, establishing, and maintaining good credit; personal financial planning and budgeting; and counseling to assist tribal members in becoming mortgage-ready. It prepares them for the reality of homeownership as to the necessities of paying for a mortgage, insurance, taxes and maintenance expenses. CHFC also provides post-loan counseling, include ongoing individual counseling as needed to develop the skills necessary to become a successful homeowner. The counseling and education that the Home Finance Program services provide help its Native American beneficiaries become more knowledgeable, less likely to become victims of predatory lending practices, and more likely to successfully manage their personal finances to become responsible homeowners. These services are a critical tactic in our strategy to break the cycle of poverty for our member families. They empower the members to understand their home as an asset they have invested in that not only creates wealth that can be transferred from one generation to another, it is an asset that they can use throughout their life as a financial tool that helps them achieve other goals like higher education, entrepreneurial investments, large purchases such as vehicles, and debt consolidation and management, thereby preserving wealth they've accumulated through their earnings. We serve an average of 400 individuals per year through our counseling services.

The benefits of the CHFC Home Finance Program extend well beyond just the Native American program participants, into their surrounding communities. Furthermore, the CHFC provides opportunities for Choctaw tribal members and others to attain home ownership nationwide by partnering with mortgage companies that offer Section 184, FHA, VA, USDA Rural Development, and even conventional loans, well beyond our service area in southeastern Oklahoma. The tribal members to whom we extend financing services—either directly or through our private lending partners—are predominantly located in the states of Oklahoma, Texas, California, Oregon, Washington, Arkansas, and Colorado, but also in many others, and these members add to the local taxes bases by paying annual property taxes. In the Choctaw Nation's ten and a half (10½) county service area in southeastern Oklahoma alone, over $100,000 was added to local real property tax bases in 2014 by the tribal members we serve. This too has had a multiplier effect—an average of 7.5 jobs were created or sustained through each loan closing in the employment of appraisers, surveyors, title companies, and attorney services, totaling 855 new jobs annually. An even greater multiplier effect can be seen throughout the country, as the partnership of the CHFC with lenders in states that do not have tribes with their own Section 184 or similar Indian home loan guarantee programs means that the CHFC's leveraging of monies from such programs can extend those programs' effects to members in those states and likewise add to the their local tax bases, increase employment opportunities, and have other positive effects. By doing so, the CNOs positive effects are felt well beyond its service area in southeastern Oklahoma. For example, there are approximately 20,000 CNO tribal members living in the State of Texas, making it the largest tribal population in that state, and the Home Finance Program assistance services provided to those members is second only to Oklahoma.

These innovations and successes by the HACNO point to the effective good that can be done through federal Indian housing programs. They also point to reasons why Congress should timely reauthorize the NAHASDA this fiscal year.

VII. Congress Should Act Swiftly to Approve the Reauthorization of the Native American Housing Assistance and Self-Determination Act, While Fully Supporting the Negotiated Rulemaking Process for Its Implementation

Congress enacted NAHASDA in 1996, establishing the IHBG program for the benefit of American Indian and Alaska Native groups. The main goals of the bill were explained by one of its chief sponsors, Rep. Rick Lazio:

- Affirm tribal self-determination by giving tribes the ability and responsibility to strategically plan their own communities' culturally-relevant development.
- Provide the maximum amount of flexibility in the use of housing dollars, within strict accountability standards.
- Allow for innovation and local problem-solving capabilities that are crucial to the success of any community-based strategy.
- Avoid over-burdening tribes and housing authorities with excessive regulation.

The NAHASDA was last reauthorized in 2008 when Congress again reaffirmed the foregoing important purposes to be served by the legislation. That reauthorization expired on September 30, 2013.

Congress must quickly reauthorize the NAHASDA. Without the NAHASDA, it is not likely that any of the success stories from the HACNO discussed above, or from many other tribal housing authorities across the country, would have been achieved.

a. Negotiated Rulemaking Process: Keeping the Government-To-Government Relationship

In accordance with section 106 of NAHASDA, HUD originally developed the regulations for implementing the Indian Housing Block Grant with active tribal participation and using the procedures of the Negotiated Rulemaking Act of 1996, 5 U.S.C. § 561–570. The NAHASDA reauthorization legislation of 2008 amended section 106 of the NAHASDA to require HUD to initiate negotiated rulemaking. In accordance with that statutory directive, HUD provided notice in the Federal Register establishing the NAHASDA Reauthorization Act Negotiated Rulemaking Committee ("Neg-Reg Committee") and asked for tribal nominations to serve on the Committee. The final Committee consisted of 25 tribal members and 2 HUD representatives, including tribal representatives from every region of the country, state-recognized tribal representatives whose tribes are eligible for the NAHASDA funding, and the Assistant Secretary for Public and Indian Housing and the Deputy Assistant Secretary for Native American Programs. Six negotiated rulemaking sessions were held to achieve a final rule for the implementation of the 2008 NAHASDA reauthorization amendments.

Probably the most important issue tackled through negotiated rulemaking has been the development of the formula by which tribes are allocated funds under the IHBG. That formula and the negotiated rulemaking process used to achieve it are the result of countless meetings and exchanges among tribal leaders and federal officials. A carefully-constructed balance of competing interests and ideals has been reached. The formula serves the diverse tribal communities affected and tribal leaders worked hard and long with federal officials to achieve that balance. Key to that formula's effectiveness is the fact that it uses U.S. Census data to take into account the need of every tribal recipient of the NAHASDA block grant funding. Any necessary changes to that allocation formula or to any other IHBG regulation should be subjected to the same negotiated rulemaking process.

Within the reauthorization of the NAHASDA, it is not just incumbent upon, but morally, historically, and politically imperative that Congress refrain from statutorily changing features of the IHBG program funding distribution formula. Rather, those changes, if any, should be left to the tribes and the federal government to address within the context of the negotiated rulemaking process. This process has not only been used to effectively implement the NAHASDA since its inception, but it is also an irreplaceable component to achieving the original purposes of the NAHASDA set out above.

An issue currently being addressed by the Formula Neg-Reg Committee convened last year is the population data set to be used in the formula. After annual appropriations bills are enacted, the U.S. Department of Housing and Urban Development (HUD) Office of Native American Programs (ONAP) applies the IHBG formula to determine tribal distributions. HUD currently uses data from the most recent U.S. Decennial Census, projected forward to the present year using birth and death rates, to determine the population figures for the Need component of the IHBG allocation formula.

Last year, HUD planned to replace its use of U.S. Decennial Census figures in the IHBG formula with data from the Census Bureau's annual American Community Survey (ACS). The ACS is an ongoing nationwide statistical survey conducted by the U.S. Census that samples a percentage of the U.S. population on a smaller scale and compiles information every year, allowing for more up-to-date reporting of data than the Decennial Census. However, any shift in the data source likely will cause shifts in funding. Based on projected effects, some NAHASDA funding recipients also have questioned the ability of the ACS to accurately capture tribal enrollment information due to alleged issues with sampling, response, and inclusion rates.

The Formula Neg-Reg Committee that convened last year researched and discussed these data set issues and put forward a unanimous proposal to address it. Under the proposal:

- Use of U.S. Census data will continue through the FY 2017 allocation.

- A study group within the current Formula Neg-Reg Committee is carrying out a 12-month project to research relevant data sources, including the ACS and others, and how each may be used or modified for use in the IHBG allocation formula. Their research will seek to find a nationally-applicable source that optimally balances accurate assessment of actual needs, equity, minimizing disruption of tribal housing programs, practicality (including costs of implementation), and respect for tribal sovereignty.

- The Formula Neg-Reg Committee will then review the study group's findings to consider an alternate data source. Any new source would not be implemented until the FY 2018 allocation.

- Finally, when a new data source is selected, the impact it causes upon implementation (whether it be a gain or loss in funding) will be spread over time (all tribes would still be subject to any proportional increase or decrease in funding resulting from the overall level of congressional appropriations, or funding shifts caused by the ongoing annual changes in the demographic data). This proposed regulatory funding formula mechanism is deigned to function as a volatility control on individual tribal funding levels resulting from utilization of a new data source.

The CNO encourages the Administration and Congress to allow the Formula Neg-Reg Committee to conclude its review of potential data sets for use within the IHBG formula and not legislatively address this issue, as S. 710 rightly does not attempt to do. If the Neg-Reg Committee determines an alternative data set to be better than the ACS, based on the criteria above, then use of such data within the IHBG formula should be implemented by regulation. If the Neg-Reg Committee is unable to find a better alternative data set, then ACS should be used as originally planned by HUD.

While no population demographic data sets are perfect, the U.S. Decennial Census data currently used and the proposed ACS are the most accurate and reliable data sets available that are uniformly gathered nationally by an independent third party. The ACS makes up for the normally reduced sample sizes used in small populations, similar to many Native American and Alaska Native communities, by compiling estimates over several years, and according to information presented to the Formula Neg-Reg Committee by a Census Bureau representative, in these particular communities they actually increase the sample size of the surveys.

According to the U.S. Census, information from the ACS survey generates data that helps determine how more than $400 billion in federal and state funds are distributed each year. ACS data has been deemed accurate and reliable enough to support, among things, the Indian Health Care Improvement Act and the Native American Programs Act, as well other laws affecting Indian Country, such as the Civil Rights Act, the Veterans Benefits Improvement Act, Johnson O'Malley and the Workforce Investment Act. In fact, last year tribal leaders in the National Congress of American Indians adopted a resolution recognizing U.S. Census Bureau data as the most accurate data source for the Johnson O'Malley AIAN target population count.

Any attempt to require tribes and TDHEs who receive IHBG funding to collect and submit their own survey data of the AIAN populations they serve would be fraught with additional problems that likely will outweigh any benefit: (i) the financial burden of collecting such information could be enormous and shifted entirely to tribes; (ii) many tribes will not have the internal administrative capacity, expertise, or manpower to carry out their own data collections; and (iii) many tribes and TDHEs serve not only their own tribal members but other American Indians and Alaska Natives within their service areas from whom no more accurate data is likely to be gathered.

Rather than completely scrapping use of ACS data even if a better data set is not recommended by the Formula Neg-Reg Committee, the CNO would suggest that HUD and the U.S. Census Bureau collaborate with tribes to consider ways to improve ACS implementation, and thereby improve its accuracy. As an example, in addition to asking for racial and ethnic identification, the survey also could request the tribal affiliation of those who identify as AIAN. Improving ACS implementation, rather than reinventing the data set wheel, is the best and most cost effective path to follow if the Formula Neg-Reg Committee does not find a better alternative.

The reason the negotiated rulemaking process generally, and the funding formula developed through that process in particular, must be kept in place is clear: the federal government has long since (and correctly) acknowledged that tribal representatives are the best decision-makers for policy choices that affect tribal communities, and even though the federal government has a trust responsibility towards tribes, that responsibility is best carried out by encouraging and supporting the government-to-government relationship between tribes and the federal government. That is exactly what the negotiated rulemaking process does—it allows representatives from tribes and tribal housing authorities to engage one another over the programmatic rules that govern their day-to-day operations, with federal representatives at the table to provide input, but most importantly, to listen and incorporate the tribal input into the final rule. This is exactly the type of scenario contemplated by Rep. Lazio and other original sponsors of NAHASDA legislation, because the negotiated rulemaking process without a doubt enables tribes to plan their community development, provides flexibility in the expenditure of resources while maintaining accountability for the good of all of Indian Country, encourages and spreads innovation among tribal representatives, and avoids unnecessary and irrelevant regulation.

With the foregoing in mind, the timely reauthorization of the NAHASDA, with the allocation formula negotiated rulemaking in place to address any necessary substantive changes, should be one of Congress's top priorities before the end of this fiscal year.

VIII. Possible Refinements to the NAHASDA Reauthorization Act of 2015

NAHASDA has undoubtedly improved the housing situation in Indian Country. However, like any national legislation aimed at addressing chronic and overarching problems in Indian Country, the NAHASDA Reauthorization Act of 2015 can be refined slightly for better results. From my perspective as a stakeholder responsible for executing delivery of services and overall grant management I respectfully offer the following suggested refinement for your consideration.

Section 301, Effect of Undisbursed Block Grant Amounts on Annual Allocations, reallocates to other IHBG recipients the excess of undisbursed block grants for a recipient if the amount in HUD's line of credit control system is greater than 3 times the formula allocation the recipient would otherwise receive for that fiscal year. This provision, although included with the right intent, should be clarified to make explicit that the statute is referencing the *sum of the recipient's last three years of IHBG grant awards,* in order to best protect the recipient from unforeseeable consequences in the event of the need for an overall appropriation reduction in any particular year. Such an event is beyond the control of those responsible for planning, managing, and timely execution of the delivery of services to ensure drawdown rates are within identified thresholds. Using the sum of the previous three years' grant allocation amount is based on known variables that ensure accountability without the chance of punitive action for circumstances beyond the control of the recipient. Further, this language creates a mechanism that adjusts the amount annually if the overall appropriation goes up or down. It also provides adequate time to recalibrate drawdown rates.

IX. Conclusion

Thank you Chairman Barrasso, Vice Chairman Tester, and members of the Senate Committee on Indian Affairs for allowing me to testify here today regarding S. 710, the Native American Housing Assistance and Self-Determination Reauthorization Act of 2015. Your continued support of our efforts, including a speedy reauthorization of NAHASDA, is truly appreciated, and I and my staff at the Housing Authority of the Choctaw Nation of Oklahoma stand ready to assist you in any way that we can.

This concludes my testimony. I would be glad to answer any questions you may have.

The CHAIRMAN. Thank you, Mr. Sossamon.

We will start with Senator Lankford.

Senator LANKFORD. Thank all of you for your preparation and excellent testimony. That were all written out in advance and all your testimony as well.

Mr. Cooper, 16 years as Executive Director of the Housing Authority of the Cherokee Nation, and now you have a national focus as well, so you are bringing a couple different lenses. I know today you represent the national focus as well.

Let me ask a question from a national look. Where do we find success? The housing issues have multiplied all over the Nation and have been a bad situation for a long time. Where do we find success in this that we can use as models or examples? Where would you point and say this is working well and why?

Mr. COOPER. I think there are a lot places you can look to find some success as Rusell mentioned. Russell has done a lot of things down in his area, in the Choctaw Nation. I think we can look at and go to several different parts of the Country to find that.

That is one of the key factors behind NAHASDA, the self-determination piece. It allows folks to determine what the best needs are for their area.

Senator LANKFORD. Give me a couple examples of that. What have you seen? I know there is not a one size fits all, we have hundreds of tribes and there is uniqueness in each. Are you finding any trends that say when this occurs, it seems to be more successful in housing?

Mr. COOPER. Earlier this year, Chairman Barrasso and this Committee had a hearing on leveraging. That has seemed to make a huge difference on it. Several of us do it in Oklahoma, it has worked well in the northwest, it has worked for our folks in Senator Murkowski's State of Alaska and for a lot of other places throughout the Country. It is the ability to leverage our Federal NAHASDA dollars with Section 183 loan dollars, with ICDBG dollars, and tax credits, for example, are another, low income housing tax credits where we can put several different pieces together and develop a housing program that meets our needs.

One of the things we see in this bill, for instance, the section that deals with the environmental review component. Before, if we and our members had four different pieces, we have to do four different environmentals. If you put other sources of funding with that, you put stuff on top of that.

Most of our and our members' time was spent doing environmentals rather than getting services out to our folks.

Whenever we are able to leverage funds, whenever we have the ability to do that, I think that is probably one of the best things I can think of that really allows our members to do other things.

Senator LANKFORD. How do you define success in the housing? When you deal with any tribe, with any entity, how do you know a program is successful?

Mr. COOPER. Whenever we are able to help our Indian families. As Chairwoman Diver mentioned, you do not hear a lot, and we do not have an issue with homelessness in Indian Country as the term "homelessness" exists for public housing or other things.

Our issue in Indian Country is with overcrowding and several families living under the same roof. We do not kick our people out on the street. Families take their folks in.

Senator LANKFORD. You take care of your folks.

Mr. COOPER. We take care of our folks.

Senator LANKFORD. Mr. Sossamon, let me ask you a quick question. I have one minute left.

You spent a lot of time both in your written testimony and your oral testimony talking about the home loan finance corporation you have set up and the shared funds, and getting people into home ownership. How has that worked? Why did that end up being a focus of the Choctaw Nation to head in that direction?

Obviously that was an intentional decision. There is a lot of paperwork involved to do that. Why and what have you seen as a result?

Mr. COOPER. It allows us to utilize those funds time and time again because as they are loaned out, they come back in and can be used again. At some point, it won't require additional new investment dollars; it will become a self-sustaining, revolving fund that not only is available to meet the mortgage needs but will cover the operational expense to provide the program.

Also, it works with our member and empowers them because they qualify, each member individually qualifies for a certain amount based on their income and their situation. If they cannot qualify, we provide counseling and education to them to point out exactly what the barriers are in their circumstance and provide them information and guidance they need to overcome the barriers they are experiencing.

Once they have overcome those barriers, and I have seen it many times, they overcome those barriers and they have that feeling of success, then they purchase that home and going through the process of purchasing or having one constructed, knowing they have earned the ability to do that makes them understand more the value of that home.

Senator LANKFORD. Thank you.

Mr. Chairman, I yield back.

The CHAIRMAN. Thank you, Senator Lankford.

Senator Tester.

Senator TESTER. Thank you, Mr. Chairman.

This is a question for Chairwoman Diver. We have been trying to break down silos and have been somewhat successful between IHS and VA but still have a ways to go.

When it comes to housing, you have silos with housing, veterans services, and human services. How successful have you been to break down those silos, number one?

Ms. DIVER. Fairly well. One of the things that is working for us in terms of supportive housing is that we use our clinical facilities and our self-governed medical facilities with integrated social services and behavioral health to provide the case management to our tenants and supportive housing.

The case management portion does not have to come out of our NAHASDA dollars; it is funded from our public health department. We can bring a host of resources to the table with the Indian Health Service or our third party billing dollars that we have created ourselves to provide comprehensive case management.

From behavioral health services, nutrition planning, public health nursing, and so forth, we then do the referrals back into either our own system or the VA as necessary, or any other community-based service.

Senator TESTER. Is there a mechanism by which you can talk about your successes to other tribes so they can replicate what you are doing to get more bang for the buck?

Ms. DIVER. I am a member of the Board of Trustees of the Corporation for Supportive Housing. I have been a housing developer and operator for about 25 years prior to becoming involved in tribal administration and tribal politics. I am also the President of the Minnesota Chippewa Tribe Finance Corporation.

Through those various methods, I have come to conferences put on by the Housing Council. HUD has actually invited me to different venues to provide workshops and breakout sessions on the financing and service delivery development.

A lot of it is done by people hearing about it and coming to visit and our sharing.

Senator TESTER. That is good.

Have you had a chance to take a look at this bill?

Ms. DIVER. Yes, I have.

Senator TESTER. No bill is perfect, although I am sure this one is as close to perfect as you can get. But based on your quick review of it, what would you change? We won't take offense to it.

Ms. DIVER. It is difficult because I do not have to sit in your shoes.

Senator BARRASSO. Time is limited, you know.

[Laughter.]

Ms. DIVER. I can sum it up in one word: more.

Senator TESTER. More?

Ms. DIVER. More everything; more cooperation between the Federal agencies. I try to bring in USDA money and the income guidelines through USDA are so incredibly low that I have 74 year old elders who have Social Security and a small pension and they are not eligible to get help with their roof.

They are offering them a low interest loan but they cannot afford debt service when they are 74 years old and living on $900 a month, yet they are over income.

If some of your partner agencies could adopt some of the same approaches of NAHASDA and have there be block grants and let us identify the need and the plan to serve them, then let tribes put in that plan within some parameters.

The silos, I know some tribes do not want to say that IHS dollars can be used for development of housing. If I have those funds available and there is enough to not only meet the critical needs of repairing the ones that are out there, but also perhaps there is enough money to use IHS dollars so I do not have to use NAHASDA and housing development.

There are so many competing needs for every single pot of money we have that we are almost afraid to ask you to remove some of those barriers because we are afraid you will not give us additional funds but say, now you do not need as much here because you can fund it over there.

Even though some of these are great ideas, I will admit sometimes we fear problem solving because we do not know if the alternative would be worse because it means there will be less resources.

Senator TESTER. I certainly appreciate your being here. I appreciate your perspective. I think one of the ways we can make sure to meet your needs is if people like you are vocal and talk about what is going on in the real world.

Gary Cooper, who has a great name, I have a quick question. I know I am out of time but I have a quick question for you.

Your testimony indicated NAIHC supports changes to NAHASDA regarding the maximum rent rule of 30 percent.

Mr. COOPER. Yes.

Senator TESTER. This is a two-edged sword.

Mr. COOPER. It is.

Senator TESTER. While we like tribal sovereignty and self-governance, and we all believe in that, what tenant protections are there? Let me give you an example. I am not saying this would happen.

Sometimes you have a tribal government that loses an election and they bring in a whole different clan. What protections do those folks have as far as their rents go, if this 30 percent rule isn't in there?

Mr. COOPER. I think that is an excellent question. Off the top of my head, I really cannot think of what protections exist. I think there might be some things that we could do to help you with that protection.

Senator TESTER. I will just say this. We want to cut red tape, we want to cut excess baloney out of this and if you can help us make sure there is some protection for these folks in here, I think we can get a win-win out of this.

Thank you very much, Mr. Cooper. Mr. Sossamon, I will leave others to grill you, but thank you very much for being here.

The CHAIRMAN. Thank you very much, Vice Chairman Tester.

Senator Franken.

Senator FRANKEN. Thank you, Mr. Chairman.

Thank you, Chairwoman Karen Diver. You are a good friend and you do a great job representing Fond du Lac and all of Minnesota's tribes and bands.

I think this is an early step towards reauthorizing NAHASDA and I am sure we will work this out as we go through the process. I look forward to working with you, Mr. Chairman and Vice Chairman Tester on this.

I want to focus on something you have done, Chairwoman Diver, in focusing on veteran homelessness because the definition of homelessness in Indian Country is doubling up and overcrowding but with veterans there is real homelessness.

Can you explain how allowing tribes to administer HUD–VASH will improve the efforts to end homelessness among our veterans among Native Americans?

Ms. DIVER. We were very supportive of HUD handling the VASH vouchers over the VA because the VA does not have a history of working with tribes at that level in administering programs on the ground.

In fact, they signed their first MOU with IHS only like two years ago, so those relationships are not established. HUD is better about understanding self-governance and decisions regarding how to deliver services to our communities are best made in our home communities, self-determination and meeting the outcomes of our citizens.

One of the key factors is understanding that tribes need to be able to define their own homelessness. I also have veterans that are at risk of homelessness. I would like to be able to serve them as well.

Being able to work with HUD and submit plans from a tribal perspective to tell them what do our veterans look like and how do we serve them best is something that was very important to us.

We are supportive of working with HUD. We have offered them commentary as they are seeking that in their rulemaking and look forward to them deploying those resources in June.

Senator FRANKEN. Let us move to the issue of overcrowding, which is homelessness, really, as you experience it in Indian Country. This creates a whole host of problems, as you wrote in your written testimony, for kids who are exposed to a lot of stuff. They may be exposed to domestic violence and drugs and alcohol. A 2012 report by Wilder Research found that overcrowding "threatens"—this is about kids—"their educational success, health, mental health and personal development."

Can you comment further on how lack of quality, affordable housing affects outcomes in education and other areas? This is for anyone.

Ms. DIVER. Certainly we saw with our homeless families, as I mentioned in my oral testimony, changing school districts, what we see happening as families who will take you in and then the stresses of having additional people in the house, usually it is time limited so that gets to be a very mobile situation where housing is only stable for three to four months at the time.

It certainly exacerbates other social ills like chemical dependency and violence. We actually started in some of our police incident reports whether or not they noted if there were families living in the housing and whether there was overcrowding conditions so we could start to make some statistics available, whether it was Justice money or some of the other sources.

It is very noteworthy that they do tend to receive more police calls. We do tend to see more contact with social services. We do tend to see more truancy. In terms of long term, academic outcomes and all of the other social indicators, it is particularly stressful on the children and hard on the parents too.

We were finding out that we were taking about 90 requests to change bus locations every single day for our transit service serving our K–12 school. They were calling on that day to either have their child picked up or dropped off in a different location.

It was actually creating some safety concerns on the part of our transit department about who was going to be there to pick up the child, what if there was no one there, what if they forget and drop them off at the previous location. It did not get on the list. There are too many ways to list, Senator Franken, of the ways that does harm to children.

Senator FRANKEN. My time has run out but if anyone else would like to amplify on that, would that be okay, Mr. Chairman? well, thank you.

The CHAIRMAN. Senator Heitkamp.

Senator HEITKAMP. Thank you, Mr. Chairman.

Getting back to the point that Senator Lankford was making and I think Senator Tester, which is you all have been patching together on each one of these reservations a series of programs to try and expand the resource and basically leverage the resource.

This really is directed at you, Mr. Cooper. When you look at the national organization, do you have a best practices, innovation kind of document that we can look at where we have seen amazing results through the creativity of sovereignty and self-determination kind of coming to the forefront saying, if we do it this way, things will happen.

I think the Chairwoman had an excellent example of how you leverage social service resources against housing resources to meet needs in housing, but I am wondering if there is something tangible we can get hold of that we can review?

Mr. COOPER. No, I do not think that we do have that. I think that is an excellent point. I know we have had this conversation a couple of times with folks over at ONAP because they also see the same and exact things we do.

They get their Indian housing plans, they will see the best practice models that might be out there. If there was some way for us to identify them, you do bring up a good point. Maybe we can look at that because that would be an excellent piece to have, the best practices of what these folks are doing in different areas.

Senator HEITKAMP. I think in cooperation with HUD, you might be able to find some resources to actually do that. I think that would be extraordinarily helpful for us, recognizing there may be a hesitancy because as the Chairwoman talked, once they discover how you are leveraging dollars, they may say oh, stop that, that is not going to happen.

That is not our goal here. Our goal here is to try and encourage some good best practices on reservations.

I want to talk to you, Mr. Sossamon, about the work you are doing with mortgage financing. I had the experience of running the State housing finance agency when I was the attorney general of North Dakota.

We worked tirelessly for four years to try and get one project in Indian Country that financed first-time homeowners. We were never able to do it because of the model of what happens with trust property. Obviously we are concerned about that.

Is there any advice you can give us on working with the mortgage lenders, working with banks, things you have seen in your experience that could be taken to reservations about leveraging private funds?

Mr. SOSSAMON. From my perspective, I believe it comes down to having good tribal laws in place on the reservation trust areas. In our particular area and in most of Oklahoma's Indian areas, we do business on fee simple lands, which are governed by the laws of the State. Therefore, the investors, not only the homebuyer investing in a home but then the private capital made available to loan to that homebuyer, need those laws in place to mitigate the risk of loss of their capital, and their resources and investment.

Senator HEITKAMP. I think that is an easier model than developing private housing that can be basically mortgage ready. Mr. Cooper, maybe you can help me in talking about the difficulty or maybe it is not true anymore, the difficulty of doing mortgage financing on trust land.

Mr. COOPER. I think we still see those difficulties out there, if there was a provision in S. 710 that would extend that to a 99-year lease.

Senator HEITKAMP. Helpful.

Mr. COOPER. That is an excellent start. That is one of those things that is needed for those trust properties of members who live on reservations. Because it is hard to get folks to invest in a piece of property if there is not a guarantee there.

Senator HEITKAMP. Many times what you are missing is the opportunity bring people to the community, they will look for those mortgage opportunities off Indian Country, probably away from the community and not be participating the way those community members would participate if they were in the community.

Mr. COOPER. Absolutely.

Senator HEITKAMP. May I ask the Chairwoman if she has any insights on mortgage finance in Indian Country?

Ms. DIVER. We passed a foreclosure ordinance through our tribal courts. We work with lenders to become certified and Section 184, help them become familiar. We do not run into as many problems with having traditional mortgage banking on our reservation.

Senator HEITKAMP. After you did this, did you see an uptick in mortgages?

Ms. DIVER. Absolutely. We also see that some tribal members, especially if they are a blended family choosing to buy private land on the reservation, they also know that we are a market because we like to reclaim obviously pieces of our homeland as well.

The lease issue, for us, with the 99-year leases, we will not lease to members who are not members. We will assist them in finding another tribal buyer or the tribe will look at whether or not they want to acquire it. That does not seem to be as big an issue for us.

Senator HEITKAMP. I think as we are looking at best practices, I guess I would recommend that you look at including a section on homeownership, not just tax credits and multifamily, but really looking at that all important homeownership that helps build communities and economies.

Thank you all. This is such a critical issue. I really appreciate your testimony.

Mr. Chairman, I appreciate so much that you are making this a top priority as we come into the 114th Congress.

The CHAIRMAN. Thank you very much, Senator Heitkamp.

Following up on that, Chairwoman Diver, it seems to me a lack of adequate housing can hinder a community's opportunity for overall economic growth. Energy development requires adequate infrastructure for housing policies in order to build and retain a work force, with housing being such a key.

Instituting local standards for housing can be an important means by which a community can actually achieve its goals.

As a tribal leader, can you explain to the Committee and for the record, the connection between tribally-established housing policies and community priorities like economic growth?

Ms. DIVER. You are absolutely right. The whole purpose of publicly-financed housing is to do community development, not just to provide a house. It is to provide wellness for communities in a very holistic way.

Being in a rural community, the Fond du Lac Band is the second largest employer in northern Minnesota with 2,200 employees, yet we are a tribe of 4,200. We have a hard time providing affordable housing for our work force, tribal and non-tribal.

Right now, we are in the Duluth-Superior metropolitan statistical area and market rate rents actually will run higher than a mortgage but yet a lot of our tribal members do not qualify for mortgages because of credit issues and so forth.

That is one of the focuses of what we are trying to do but our NAHASDA money is make people homeowner ready. That is one of the reasons why we have down payment assistance programs and things like that.

A lack of affordable housing is not just in our area provided by the tribe. It is in the region. It is underfunded, not just for tribes, although more underfunded for tribes than other PHAs. It is affecting economic development upwards in terms of work force development and, as I said earlier, all of those other social stressors that come with families in crisis.

The CHAIRMAN. Thank you.

Mr. Cooper, government-to-government dealings, I think, is an important part of the Federal-tribal relationship. In addition to your serving on the National American Indian Housing Council board, you also served on a NAHASDA formula negotiated rule-making.

Mr. COOPER. Yes, Mr. Chairman.

The CHAIRMAN. That committee was a government-to-government body deliberating regulations governing formula allocation. One of the issues the group addressed was the matter of undispersed funds.

I am wondering if you could explain to the Committee how the government-to-government body approached this work. After your deliberations, what did the tribal and Federal government representatives resolve in terms of undispersed funds?

Mr. COOPER. I think that is a good question if for no other reason than it stresses the importance of that government-to-government piece. If this bill passes and we get to negotiated rulemaking on this bill, then I think there is also a chance maybe we can put some of those protections in place that Vice Chairman Tester talked about that might be needed.

Back to your question with the undispersed funds, it is an issue. We sat down and discussed it. As far as the language we proposed, it was very close other than a few technical differences, mirrors exactly what you put in the bill that I see in front of me here today.

Of course I am the younger person on the committee. I think Russell served on a few more than I, but that was my first experience. It is a process that does work. Everyone sits down at the table and we all come to a consensus, we all come to agreement on the final product.

The CHAIRMAN. One of the things Senator Tester asked about had to do with tribal elections. I was wondering, as a tribal housing official, could you explain how the relationship exists between elected officials and housing administrators which I believe are governed by charters and other forms of legal oversight and the accountability there?

Mr. COOPER. In a lot of places, there is that issue where the housing folks are also the housing department of the tribe. I could give a little history and Russell could probably give more than I ever could.

The housing authority had to be separate. The Indian Housing Authority was a separate entity outside of the tribe prior to NAHASDA. When NAHASDA came about, the tribes could take over that. Either the Indian Housing Authority or the tribe could become the tribally-designated housing entity.

It is kind of one of those mixed barrels. You have places where theoretically it could happen where elections could play a part and in other places, it may not have any effect on it but that does differ. That is really one of the ways it does.

The CHAIRMAN. Mr. Sossamon, do you have anything you want to add to that?

Mr. SOSSAMON. As far as the relationships, particularly at Choctaw, my board of commissioners are appointed by my Chief and confirmed by my Council. There is accountability to the tribal government.

Beyond that, NAHASDA recognizes the tribe as the primary beneficiary of NAHASDA funds and they chose by government action to name the housing authority as their designated entity.

If the entity is not responsive to the needs as identified by the elected officials of the government, they simply act and remove that designation and they no longer receive those funds.

The CHAIRMAN. S. 710 provides tribes with tools to address their unique circumstances and meet their goals. One of the sections enhances tribes' leasing authority. Another section provides more streamlined and predictable environmental review processes. Another section includes tribally-designated housing entities as qualifying community-based development organizations. Another section promotes leveraging of NAHASDA funds.

Can you share with the Committee how this bill will help tribes attract development project partners? Because it is not just about a house, it is about the future, economic development, education, health and the overall well being. And what impact will those partnerships have on the quality of life that the Choctaw Nation's citizens could enjoy?

Mr. SOSSAMON. Basically, all of these provisions create a multitude of new options available to us to look at in every community and the environment in which we want to do a development, much like a private developer does.

They have to have the flexibility to put together whatever pieces are necessary to be successful in developing in an area. This will allow tribal housing professionals to look at things more like a market type developer would.

It gives us the flexibility to really assess what it is going to take in this area which may not be exactly the same as what it takes in this area, but previous to that, government programs tried to be as Mr. Cooper pointed out, cookie cutters and one size fits all.

We know in the real market, that is not how it works. The closer we can get to operating the way the real market does, the more likely it is that private market investors and developers are going to come in and work with us.

The CHAIRMAN. It does not appear there are any more questions. The hearing record will be open for two weeks. Other members may submit written questions.

I want to thank all of you for being here, for your time and testimony today.

The hearing is adjourned.

[Whereupon, at 3:48 p.m., the Committee was adjourned.]

APPENDIX

PREPARED STATEMENT OF LOURDES CASTRO RAMIREZ, PRINCIPAL DEPUTY ASSISTANT SECRETARY FOR PUBLIC AND INDIAN HOUSING, U.S. DEPARTMENT OF HOUSING AND URBAN DEVELOPMENT

Good Afternoon Chairman Barrasso, Vice Chairman Tester, and Members of the Committee. Thank you for inviting the U.S. Department of Housing and Urban Development (HUD) to testify on S. 710, a bill to reauthorize the Native American Housing Assistance and Self-Determination Act of 1996 (NAHASDA).

My name is Lourdes Castro Ramirez and I am the Principal Deputy Assistant Secretary for Public and Indian Housing (PIH) at HUD. PIH is responsible for the management, operation, and oversight of HUD's American Indian, Alaska Native, and Native Hawaiian housing programs.

NAHASDA provides a successful approach, guided by the principles of self-determination and self-governance, to providing decent and affordable Indian housing and developing tribal economies. The Indian Housing Block Grant (IHBG), the largest program under NAHASDA, has infused almost $11.4 billion to support a range of affordable housing and community development activities in tribal communities since its inception 18 years ago.

Over the life of the program, IHBG recipients have built or acquired almost 37,000 affordable housing units in Indian Country, and substantially rehabilitated more than 73,000. IHBG recipients also currently maintain more than 46,000 "HUD units" that were funded before NAHASDA was enacted.

HUD is very pleased that the reauthorization of NAHASDA is a priority for this Committee. HUD strongly supports the reauthorization of NAHASDA because the law is essential to furthering housing opportunities and building sustainable communities throughout Indian Country.

We are currently reviewing and analyzing S. 710 and welcome the opportunity to work with the Committee and staff to provide recommendations on several existing provisions, as well as offer insight on ways to further improve NAHASDA.

Today, I would like to share with you our initial views on the draft bill. First I will comment on the provisions included in the bill, and then discuss some other concepts HUD would like to see reflected in the bill.

HUD appreciates the Committee's support for addressing the needs of homeless veterans on reservations. HUD is actively working with the Department of Veterans Affairs on developing a tribal HUD-Veterans Affairs Supportive Housing (HUD–VASH) demonstration program as authorized in the Consolidated and Further Continuing Appropriations Act of 2015. The implementation and evaluation of this demonstration should help inform the discussion around how best to address the problem, and we look forward to sharing the results of the demonstration with this Committee.

HUD also understands the desire of this Committee and IHBG recipients to streamline environmental reviews. We appreciate the Committee's attempt to address this vexing issue. As directed by Senate Report 113–182, HUD is working with other Federal agencies to coordinate and streamline environmental reviews involved in Indian housing development. This working group will issue a report to Congress with recommendations on how to streamline the current process. And finally, HUD is encouraged to see the Committee bill supporting the reauthorization of the Indian Home Loan Guarantee Program and the Native Hawaiian Homeownership Act.

While we are still reviewing the bill in its entirety, I would like to share some initial reactions to proposed amendments to several sections of NAHASDA included in S. 710. First, proposed amendments to Section 104 would further loosen already flexible requirements regarding the use of program income. Currently, program income can be spent on any housing or housing-related activities, and is not subject to any other Federal requirements. HUD does not support this language as proposed, because it would loosen existing requirements even further, and would allow funds generated from the use of program income to be used for any purposes with no restrictions, including purposes wholly unrelated to housing.

The changes proposed in Section 201 would impact the affordability of NAHASDA units and change the nature of a program originally targeted to low-income families. The bill as drafted would allow recipients to charge rents that exceed 30 percent of area median income with a simple written policy. This erodes the Department's goal of ensuring that rent payments remain affordable, and may significantly increase rent burdens on low-income Indian families. HUD believes compromise language may be possible that would address the need for higher rents in some circumstances, while protecting the long-term affordability of NAHASDA housing units.

The Department is also concerned about the provision proposed in Section 202. The provision would authorize a de minimis exemption to the affordability period currently applicable for the useful life of a unit funded with NAHASDA funds—further diluting the affordability of NAHASDA programs. If the period of affordability is eliminated for these units, the property could be sold at a higher cost to over-income families shortly after the rehabilitation is complete.

Finally, we understand there are concerns from Indian tribes requesting approval to exceed total development costs (TDC), and the desire to have additional flexibility when projects may exceed TDC. Under current law, IHBG recipients are able to exceed TDC by 10 percent without HUD approval. If recipients wish to exceed the 10 percent cap, under the current regulations, they may seek a variance from HUD. The proposed amendment would provide recipients the authority to exceed TDCs up to 20 percent over the TDC limit without prior HUD approval. It is our understanding that this language has been included to allow for variances caused by the use of sustainable green building practices. HUD supports sustainable practices. However, we need to carefully balance this goal with the equally important goal of preventing the investment of IHBG funds into a few, high-cost homes instead of dedicating the funds to producing more, affordable housing units.

HUD also welcomes the opportunity to work with the Committee on changes to NAHASDA to reflect the following concepts:

- Enrich the type of data reported by recipients, including data on energy efficiency, construction costs, and level of assistance provided to elders and veterans.
- Strengthen insurance requirements to better protect NAHASDA investments.
- Preserve the intent of NAHASDA by ensuring that homes are conveyed to families as intended.
- Protect NAHASDA funds in emergency situations.
- Permanently authorize refinancing in the Native Hawaiian Housing Loan Guarantee Program.

We look forward to working with the Committee and staff to refine S. 710 to support the goal we share of meeting the affordable housing needs of American Indian and Alaska Native families, and playing an integral part in building sustainable Indian communities. Thank you.

PREPARED STATEMENT OF NADINE ENCINO, SENIOR OPERATIONS SPECIALIST, LAGUNA
HOUSING DEVELOPMENT AND MANAGEMENT ENTERPRISE

I am Nadine Encino, the Chief of Operations for Laguna Housing Development &
Management Enterprise. Thank you Chairman Barrasso and other members of the
Senate Committee on Indian Affairs, for considering improvements to the Native
American Housing Assistance and Self-Determination Act (NAHASDA) as part of
Reauthorization, an issue of great importance to Indian Country. We write to provide the
Committee additional information regarding S.710's proposed amendments to
NAHASDA that we strongly support and believe will benefit both the United States and
Indian Country.

Section 205(a)

Two proposed amendments to Section 205(a) of NAHASDA (25 U.S.C. § 4135)
will improve community stability, as well as reduce administrative burdens without
sacrificing accountability. The first provision adds Subparagraph E to Section 205(a)(1),
permitting a resident family to purchase its rental unit if the family residing in the home
was eligible at the time of initial occupancy. This promotes community stability by
permitting a resident family, that initially needed housing assistance, to remain in and
own the same home when its finances improve.

The second proposed amendment adds language to Section 205(c) to help reduce
administrative burdens on Tribally-Designated Housing Entities (TDHEs) while
maintaining reasonable protections for affordable housing funds. NAHASDA prohibits
the transfer of a housing unit (constructed or assisted with Indian Housing Block Grant
funds) to a non-low-income family during the housing unit's "useful life." The proposed
amendment would relieve a TDHE of monitoring compliance with the "useful life"
transfer restriction in cases in which the assisted housing unit is privately-owned as long
as the costs of such assistance do not exceed 10% of the unit's Total Development Cost
(TDC). The use of 10% of the TDC value, rather than a dollar amount, accommodates
the disparities in housing construction costs throughout Indian Country. This amendment
would relieve the TDHE from useful life restrictions when services are provided to low-
income families residing in private homes as long as such services are moderate.
However, it would not be applicable once the cost of services exceeds 10% of TDC.

99-year Lease

A proposed amendment to Section 502 of NAHASDA (25 U.S.C. § 4211) will increase the maximum term of a lease for residential or housing development purposes from 50 years to 99 years. This helps a homebuyer to stay in possession of the housing unit during his/her lifetime, and reduces administrative burdens for the TDHE. We are grateful for the increased flexibility.

30% Rule

Proposed amendments to Section 203 of NAHASDA (25 U.S.C. § 4133) will permit a TDHE to establish rental caps in excess of the current maximum, which is 30% of a resident family's adjusted income (30% Rule). From the 1940s to the 1960s, maximum rents could not exceed 20% of income. The maximum rent increased to 25% of income in 1969, and increased to 30% in 1981. In many areas of Indian Country, the 30% Rule operates as a barrier to sustainable housing development because of higher on-reservation development costs. The proposed amendment retains the 30% Rule as a threshold standard but permits flexibility in tribal programs to address local variables in development cost and family income. As long as the TDHE has a written policy governing maximum rents and homebuyer payments, the 30% Rule would not apply. The proposed amendment not only addresses development cost disparities across Indian Country but also promotes tribal self-determination.

Conclusion

We support the proposed language changes in S.710 and ask for your support, too. We are quite anxious to see the reauthorization of NAHASDA, which has been lingering for two years now. Thank you for the opportunity to submit this testimony to assist the Committee in its deliberation.